Comprehensive Services to Rural Poor Families

Keith Baker
Myfanway Glasso
Don Goyette
C. Freemont Sprague

The Praeger Special Studies program—
utilizing the most modern and efficient book
production techniques and a selective
worldwide distribution network—makes
available to the academic, government, and
business communities significant, timely
research in U.S. and international economic, social, and political development.

Comprehensive Services to Rural Poor Families
An Evaluation of the Arizona Job Colleges Program

PRAEGER SPECIAL STUDIES IN U.S. ECONOMIC, SOCIAL, AND POLITICAL ISSUES

Praeger Publishers New York Washington London

Library of Congress Cataloging in Publication Data
Main entry under title:

Comprehensive services to rural poor families.

   (Praeger special studies in U.S. economic, social,
and political issues)
   Bibliography: p.
   Includes index.
   1. Social service, Rural—Arizona. 2. Family
social work—Arizona. I. Baker, Keith.
HV98. A6C65   362. 8'2'09791   75-36414
ISBN 0-275-56310-3

PRAEGER PUBLISHERS
111 Fourth Avenue, New York, N.Y. 10003, U.S.A.

Published in the United States of America in 1976

Printed in the United States of America

This volume is the culmination of a three and one-half year evaluation study of AJC begun by the firm of Systems, Science, and Software of La Jolla, California, under Office of Economic Opportunity Contract #B00-5192 and completed by the firm of Policy Development Consultants, La Jolla, California, under the Department of Labor Contract #P.O. 43-4-003-06. The views put forth in this document are the sole responsibility of the authors and do not necessarily represent the official policy of either the Department of Labor or the Office of Economic Opportunity (now the Community Services Administration).

The authors would like to thank the following, without whose help and assistance this report would not have been possible: at the Arizona Job Colleges, Dr. Louis Nau, Sid Goodman, Gary Bellrichard, Jack Baer, the AJC staff and trainee families; at the Office of Economic Opportunity, Norman Gold, Ethel Overby, Dr. Morris Shepard, and Rena Thompson; at the Department of Labor, Dr. George Daugherty; and Jan Tourmainen and Irma Johns for their excellent secretarial assistance.

CONTENTS

LIST OF TABLES

LIST OF FIGURES

LIST OF ABBREVIATIONS

ABE	Adult Basic Education Program
ADC	Aid to Dependent Children
AEC	Arizona Ecumenical Council
AJC	Arizona Job Colleges
ASDH	Arizona State Department of Health
BIA	Bureau of Indian Affairs
CAC	Central Arizona College
CADA	Choanoke Area Development Association
CAP	Community Action Program
CDC	Child Development Center
CEP	Concentrated Employment Program
DES	Arizona Department of Employment Security
DOL	Department of Labor
DVR	Arizona Department of Vocational Rehabilitation
ESL	English as a Second Language
FAA	Federal Aviation Administration
FHA	Federal Housing Administration
GED	General Education Development Test
GRCC	Gila River Career Center
HEW	Department of Health, Education, and Welfare
HSMHA	Health Services and Mental Health Administration
HUD	Department of Housing and Urban Development
JDP	Job Development and Placement
JOBS	Job Opportunities in the Business Sector
LARC	Local Alcoholic Rehabilitation Center
MDTA	The Manpower Development Training Act (job training programs funded under MDTA)
MHS	Migrant Health Service
MOP	Migrant Opportunity Program
NYC	Neighborhood Youth Corps
OEO	Office of Economic Opportunity
OJT	On-job Training
OPD	Office of Program Development
PCC	Parent-Child Center
PCHA	Pinal County Housing Authority
PCPHS	Pinal County Public Health Services
PT&T	Pacific Telephone and Telegraph Company
RSA	Rehabilitative Services Administration
SRA	Science Research Associates
SRS	Social and Rehabilitation Service
T&VE	Testing and Vocational Evaluation unit
TOJ	Training on the Job
UTETC	United Tribes Employment Training Center
VISTA	Volunteers in Service to America
WIN	Work Incentive Program

Comprehensive Services to Rural Poor Families

CHAPTER 1

COMPREHENSIVE RESIDENTIAL FAMILY
REHABILITATION PROGRAMS

Arizona Job Colleges, Inc. (AJC) is a comprehensive residential family rehabilitation program serving rural poor families in south-central Arizona. AJC provides its client families with vocational training, basic education, home living skills training, job placement services, and a variety of supportive services such as counseling, medical care, day care, and tutoring for school-age children. The first client-families were enrolled in AJC in the summer of 1970 and, at the same time, a program evaluation was begun which extended over the first three and one-half years of AJC's operations. This study is the final report of the findings from that evaluation.

Comprehensive residential family rehabilitation programs have three characteristics that establish their uniqueness among the range of social service and manpower training programs presently in operation.

First, comprehensive social and training-related services are provided. In many ways it is inappropriate to speak of a social or manpower training system in the United States today. Instead, we are confronted by a nonsystem, by a crazy-quilt patchwork of a variety of programs, which are sometimes complimentary but may also be duplicative, contradictory, and confusing. Social service programs are offered by local, state, and federal levels of government, and by private organizations. At the federal level, as narrowly a defined category of social service programs as job training may be provided by the Community Services Administration (formerly the office of Economic Opportunity), the Office of Education, the National Institute of Education, the Department of Labor, the Defense Department, the Department of Justice, and probably, by many other organs.

On the one hand, then, we have a society whose social service system is complex and confusing, and on the other hand, we have the target of all this activity, the poor.

1

While an exhaustive review of the literature on the problems of the poor is beyond the scope of this study (see Ferman et al. 1965 for an overall review), we would call attention to the fact that American social theorizing generally holds that the poor have more problems than poverty in itself. The problems of the poor also include poor health, lack of education, lack of knowledge of how to cope with the modern economy, language problems, racial discrimination, lack of job skills, and so on. So we find the poor person beset by a variety of problems, confronting a society that purports to offer him help with his problems but that provides that help through a service delivery system that is so complex, confusing, and scattered that it can only be through luck and perseverance that the person in need can find the required services. The idea of integrated or comprehensive social services is to rationally assemble the needed panoply of services under one roof so as to make them easily accessible (see Aries Corp. 1974 and March 1968 for a discussion of the theory).

One of the fundamental principles underlying AJC, then, is the assumption that the poor have many problems and that the most effective way of meeting their needs is through an integrated social service delivery system. The many components of the AJC service delivery system will be described in later sections.

The second unique characteristic of comprehensive residential family rehabilitation programs is that site residential facilities are provided. The rationale for providing on-site housing for the families in training has four bases. First, in sparsely settled rural areas the only feasible way to overcome the logistics of bringing trainees and services together is to concentrate the services at a single site with housing for the clients, who are drawn from a large geographic area (Aries Corp. 1974). Second, a residential program facilitates the effectiveness of the training program. "The residential method affords tighter case control, greater structure and coordination of program elements, development of a sense of esprit de corps, and an environment relatively free from outside distractions and interference" (Nau 1973a). Third, a residential program removes the client from a home environment which may be so culturally deprived or disorganized that whatever gains result from spending part of a day at the training site are destroyed when the client returns to his negative home environment (Aries Corp. 1974). Fourth, assuming the vocational training program is a success and the client moves into the economic mainstream, he will be able to afford much better housing. As will be shown below, after leaving AJC, AJC's client-families typically progress from living in the desert in overcrowded, dirt-floored shacks lacking plumbing, to typical lower-middle-class homes. The family must therefore be able to make a successful adjustment to a radically different style of life. How is the newly upwardly-mobile housewife going to know how to properly care for linoleum in the kitchen, tile in the bathroom, and carpets in the living room, when her whole prior experience has been with dirt floors? The residential program component can be used to expose the family to a new and different lifestyle, under controlled conditions that will lead to its being able to successfully cope with it (see AJC 1969).

The focus of a program of family rehabilitation is the family, rather than the breadwinner. Again, several lines of thought contributed to the development of this concept. "One is that program which attempts to move a person out of poverty without preparing his family to accompany him labors under a severe handicap"(AJC 1969, p. 2). Just as a rising young executive may find his career at a standstill as a result of his spouse's lack of social graces, so might a poor farmer be held back from moving into the lower middle class by his poor farmer's wife. A closely related phenomenon is the problem of the breadwinner outgrowing his spouse. The classic middle-class case is the rising young executive with a homebound suburban wife and mother. One day they discover that she knows nothing about what he does and that he no longer is interested in her suburban housewife's day. This drifting apart of lifestyles results in severe stress on the family, often ending in divorce. But should we expect any less social stress on the poor family upwardly mobile from a shack in the desert to the lower middle class? If the family is not prepared to adjust to new lifestyles, it may not survive the climb out of poverty, or, alternatively, economic mobility may be sacrificed to preserve family solidarity. A second line of thought is the question of the focus of antipoverty efforts. Is poverty a condition of families or of individuals? An antipoverty program that is only concerned with the breadwinner assumes either that the rehabilitation of the breadwinner will result in the rehabilitation of the family or that only the breadwinner has problems. Family rehabilitation assumes that the problems of poverty are family problems and that successful antipoverty programs must deal with the entire family, not just the breadwinner, as the unit of treatment. A second line of thought is the following:

> The concept of family rehabilitation is based upon the premise that when a disability strikes, every other member of that family is also adversely affected.[*] Thus, it is postulated that disability is rarely simple when present with or aggravated by other family-oriented problems. Rehabilitation services in such cases must be intensive and comprehensive, designed and delivered in a manner to meet the disability needs of the family, as well as the disabilities of individual members. (Nau 1973a)

---

[*] In Nau's terminology "disability" refers to the family head being poor.

EXISTING PROGRAMS[*]

By comparison to the overall size of the piecemeal social
service delivery programs, comprehensive residential family
rehabilitation programs play a very minor role in antipoverty efforts.
We have identified not more than eight such programs in the United
States in recent years, only six of which are presently in operation.
Five of these operating programs are described briefly below; the
sixth, the AJC program, is described in Chapters 2 through 7.

Mountain-Plains Program

The Mountain-Plains Family-Residential Career Education Program
is operated by the Mountain-Plains Education & Economic Development
Program, Inc., a nonprofit corporation chartered in Montana. The program is located as a tenant organization on Glasgow Air Force Base
near Glasgow, Montana. Participants in the program are drawn from
rural poor families in the states of Idaho, Montana, Wyoming, North
and South Dakota, and Nebraska. The main hypothesis underlying the
Mountain-Plains Program is that, by relocating a family away from a
poverty setting, providing a comprehensive set of educational and
other services, and assisting family heads in finding work upon completion of the program, Mountain-Plains can be effective in breaking
the cycle of rural poverty. The Mountain-Plains Program, originally
designated by the U.S. Office of Education to implement the Fourth
National Model in Career Education, is currently operated under a
contract with the national Institute of Education and is presently completing the fourth year of a five-year research and development effort.

The Mountain-Plains Program serves at any one time approximately
200 families in residence at its site on Glasgow Air Force Base. Potential participant-families are referred to Mountain-Plains by state and
private agencies, civic, church and tribal groups, and from lists of
families that have received economic or social rehabilitative services
in the past. Families are screened to see if they meet program entry
criteria. (Criteria include age, ability to work, at least a primary
education, and other points designed to limit the eligible group to
families with a reasonable chance of success.) The screening process
provides "pre-Center" information on all eligible families. One-sixth
of these families are randomly assigned to a control group. Families

---

*This section was prepared by C. F. Sprague and D. Goyette
under Contract Number NIE-C-74-1047 from the National Institute
of Education.

that enter the program begin orientation and career exploration activities
designed to identify family members' needs and produce individualized
plans for career education and other services. Participant-families
who complete the program remain in residence for an average of eight
to nine months. Program components and services provided by Mountain-
Plains include:

- career guidance, required for both the head-of-household and
  spouse
- a career development program for the head-of-household and
  optionally for the spouse, including foundation education in
  math skills and communication skills, occupational preparation,
  and work experience
- family and individual counseling for head-of-household and
  spouse and, based on need, for older children
- a family core curriculum designed to provide both head-of-
  household and spouse with home management, health, consumer
  education, parenting, community organization, and recreation
  skills
- limited basic medical, dental, and optical benefits through
  contracted services
- financial support of the family while in the program
- child development and care for pre-school-age youngsters
- placement services
- supportive follow-on services after placement

The occupational preparation component of the career development
program stresses mastery of identified essential competencies for
entry-level positions in the career areas of building trades and
services, mobility and transportation, tourism and marketing, and
office work. There are a total of approximately 50 individual careers
within the clusters identified above for which occupational preparation
is available.

In each of its required areas, the Mountain-Plains Program provides individualized diagnostic and prescriptive mechanisms for
determining sequences of instruction for each student. Plans prepared
for each student recognize already-existing skill levels as noted by
pre tests. Student progress is then monitored on a continuing basis
with formal review every six weeks or at interim points based on need.
Completion of the Mountain-Plains Program is defined as validation in
all required program areas by both adults, including the requirement
for validation in an occupational skill for the head-of-household.
Validation is based upon the achievement of competency or performance
objectives as determined by post-tests. Job placement activities
begin three months before training is completed and families are
assisted in relocating to where employment has been found. Families
terminating the program prior to completion (resignees) are also provided

placement assistance. All families leaving the program (completers and resignees) are administered follow-up interviews at six-month intervals over a two-year period. The control group families are also followed up.

The principal rationale for the existence of the Mountain-Plains Program is research and development. The operational aspect of the program—the actual implementation of the concept at Mountain-Plains— will provide information on program feasibility, cost, and practical considerations involved in providing comprehensive career education and related services to families in a residential setting.

Madera Employment Training Center

The Madera Employment Training Center is operated, for Native Americans only, by American Indian Enterprises, Inc. under contract to the Sacramento office of the Bureau of Indian Affairs (BIA). Program participants include single men and women, families, and "solo" parents (BIA terminology for unmarried women with children).

The Madera Employment Training Center is located on a former Air Force radar station about five miles outside of Madera, California, in the agricultural San Joaquin Valley. The Center covers a 56-acre site, with 27 individual two-, three-, and four-bedroom houses, three dormitories, a four-plex efficiency apartment building, a dining hall/ snack bar, an administration building, and several classroom buildings, shops, and laboratories. In addition, the Center has a number of recreational facilities, including a gymnasium, a swimming pool, a tennis court, and a baseball diamond.

There are three vocational education programs offered by the Center. Two of them, the General Facilities Equipment Technician and the Electronics Technician programs, are operated with the assistance of the U.S. Federal Aviation Administration (FAA), and are specifically designed to train students for FAA positions. The jobs for which the students in these programs are trained are technically demanding and involve a great deal of responsibility, in that the employee will be maintaining and operating vital aviation aids to navigation, often in remote areas with little direct supervision. The third program uses employees of the Pacific Telephone & Telegraph Company (PT&T) as instructors in telecommunications skills training. Completers of the PT&T program are placed in jobs within one of the Bell System companies or with the RCA Alaskan Communications Corporation. BIA reimburses PT&T for these instructors' salaries and expenses. The two FAA programs are ten months in duration and the PT&T program is ten weeks long.

The Madera Employment Training Center's capacity is about 150 students. However, during fiscal year 1974, average program participation was only 20. This underutilization is attributable to two factors. First, the tribal governing board of the student's home reservation must commit itself to paying his subsistence stipend during the training period (American Indian Enterprises covers only operating costs). These funds come out of the BIA training allotment to the tribe, and tribal governing boards are reluctant to spend portions of these allotments for activities other than their own locally-run training programs. Second, while American Indian Enterprises has the responsibility for operating the program, it does not perform the recruitment and job placement functions; these activities are carried out by BIA. BIA's approach to recruitment and job placement is to first identify a job opening and then select a potential trainee to fill the job. Only after the job opening has been identified and the employer committed to filling it is the trainee admitted to the training center. Thus conditions for entry are more restrictive than for programs which recruit first and worry about job placement later.

The Madera Employment Training Center does not provide child development or child care services to its participant-families. Thus, participation by wives in the program as trainees is not encouraged. Those wives who do participate are either childless or forced to hire nonparticipating wives as babysitters.

The day-to-day activities at the Center are informal, and staff/trainee relations are excellent. As is true with all programs of this type, the staff is dedicated to the concept of family-residential training. The BIA Sacramento Area office employment assistance specialist spends a great deal of her time at the training center and is very much an integral part of the operation. The marked lack of the paternalism often found in similar programs reflects her considerable influence and her philosophy about the operation of residential training programs. Students are expected to handle their own problems, with little coddling. For example, under American Indian Enterprises' contract, medical services are not provided, and the Center's infirmary has been closed down. A list of all the town's physicians, dentists, and so on, is provided to the trainees. Trainees are expected to arrange for their own medical services and to pay about 20 percent of their own medical costs; this simulates a typical medical insurance program associated with fulltime employment. The program has found that this policy also reduces absenteeism due to illness.

American Indian Enterprises was awarded its initial one-year contract to provide general and administrative support services to the Madera Employment Training Center in October 1972, with a contract start date of November 1, 1972. At the same time, the Inter-Tribal Council of California was awarded a one-year contract to provide instructional services at Madera Employment Training Center. These contract awards were the result of a BIA competitive procurement process. The Inter-Tribal Council's contract was not renewed by BIA, whereas the American Indian Enterprises contract was renewed, starting

November 1, 1973, on a sole-source basis. Under this new contract,
instructional services for one of the Center's major programs (the "FAA
program") are provided in addition to general and administrative support services. PT&T's Training Division also began supplying instructors in November 1973 for the "PT&T Program."

During the five years prior to the present contracting arrangement,
the Madera Employment Training Center was operated by Philco-Ford's
Education and Technical Services Division. Philco-Ford met the
requirements of its contract with respect to producing the necessary
number of trained Native Americans. However, they ultimately lost
the contract because of the "buy Indian" movement within BIA. Philco-
Ford is regarded by American Indian Enterprises and BIA staff persons
currently associated with program operations as having been paternalistic and condescending toward its program participants.

Under Philco-Ford, the Madera Employment Training Center was a
very active and overcrowded program. As of September 1971 they were
serving 250 participants (two large apartment houses in Madera were
leased to handle the overload on available dwelling units), made up of
families, singles, and solo parents, with an annual operating budget
of $2.5 million plus a fee of from 8 to 10 percent. By contract,
and as noted earlier, the program currently serves an average of about
20 participants with a budget of about $716,000. Current program staff
members criticize Philco-Ford for overselling the program to Native
Americans, in order to meet their contract requirements regarding
numbers of people trained. The result was that the program under
Philco-Ford experienced a 54 percent dropout rate, and was successful
in placing only 80 percent of its graduates in jobs.

Philco-Ford offered a variety of training programs, including
automotive/small engine repair, drafting, clerical operations, culinary
arts, electronics assembly, health occupations, appliance/radio-TV
maintenance, building trades, welding, and offset printing. Philco-
Ford originally offered only prevocational training and basic education,
and gradually added the above list of training programs to combat boredom among the program participants. All of the training courses offered
by Philco-Ford, with the exception of welding, are regarded by current
program staff members as having been low in quality, the primary
criticism being that the equipment used in the courses was obsolete
(prewar in some cases). Nevertheless, Philco-Ford, after four years
of operation, had enrolled approximately 1500 trainees, of which 650
were completers and 560 were placed in jobs.

Recent changes at BIA have had considerable impact on the Madera
Employment Training Center's operation. The contract to operate the
program was originally (in April 1967) awarded and administered by
BIA's central office in Washington, D.C. The Employment Assistance
Division of BIA contracted with large, well-known companies (Philco-
Ford, Thiokol Chemical, and Bendix Corporation) to run its employment
training centers (in Madera, Roswell, New Mexico, and Bismarck,

North Dakota, respectively). After BIA's "redirection," these contracts were not renewed. New contracts for operating the centers at
Madera and Bismarck were awarded to Native American organizations
and the center at Roswell was closed. Administration of the contract
to operate Madera was moved from Washington, D.C. to the Sacramento Area office of BIA in March 1973.

Manpower, Education and Training, Inc.

Manpower, Education and Training, Inc. is a nonprofit corporation
which operates, among a variety of other activities, a three-phase
family relocation program. This program includes a residential-
training phase which offers foundation education, prevocational training, child development services, counseling, and housing. The term
"relocation" refers to the fact that Manpower, Education and Training
participant-families are relocated from the "base area" (south Texas)
to the "placement area" (the Houston-Beaumont area).

Manpower, Education and Training was organized as a community
action program in 1967. The program's offices were originally in
Beaumont, Texas and the target population was the migrant and seasonal
farmworkers of the "Pine Belt" Region (a corridor running from Houston
to east of Dallas) of Texas. Program activities were oriented toward
retraining farm workers through placement in such programs as on-the-
job training, employment skills training, or high school equivalence
course, or through referrals to other agencies, such as the Texas
Vocational Rehabilitation Commission. By 1972, Manpower, Education
and Training had expanded its activities into the Rio Grande Valley of
Texas, and into southwest Louisiana. The administrative offices and
corporation headquarters were moved to Cleveland, Texas in order to
better coordinate the seven regional centers which had by then been
established.

The primary activity of the Goodrich, Texas center is the residential training phase of the "Total Family Relocation Program." This
program provides for outreach, recruitment, referral to the Texas
Employment Commission for certification of eligiblity for benefits,
assessment, orientation, educational and prevocational training,
supervision of relocation, supervision of on-the-job training, job
development and placement, counseling, and provision of housing
supportive services and long-range follow-up. Eligible participant-
families must:

- be farmworkers who have had to leave the home base area to
  participate in farmwork which is too far away to allow daily
  commuting from job site to home base
- have migrated the previous year in search of farmwork

- have earned at least 50 percent of their income from farmwork in the past year
- meet the most recent poverty criteria established by the Department of Labor
- express a desire to settle out of the migrant stream

The three phases of the program are described below.

For Phase I, families are recruited in the "base area," the Rio Grande Valley in south Texas. Recruiters operate out of the two Manpower, Education and Training, Inc. regional centers in Eagle Pass, Texas and Loredo, Texas. After signing up for the relocation program, a family spends about six weeks in Phase I. During this period families commute to the regional centers for orientation, assessment, counseling, life skills training, and foundation education (primarily basic English). Orientation includes slides and movies about life at the Goodrich residential center. During the orientation period counselors at the base area centers assess the family's chances of "making it" after being relocated. This six-week period also provides a time for a family to decide whether or not it really wants to participate in a training/relocation program. At the end of Phase I participant-families who are still in the program are moved from the base area to the residential center in groups of from five to seven families. Manpower, Education and Training provides for moving their household goods and each family drives to the center in their own vehicle (migrant families all have automobiles).

In Phase II, families spend eight to 12 weeks at the residential center in Goodrich. An average family's (male) head-of-household spends half-time in "prevocational" training and half-time in foundation education. Prevocational training is offered in three areas: welding, building trades, and basic auto mechanics. All training is conducted at the residential center. This training is termed "prevocational" because the program cannot offer a full-fledged, state-approved voca-ional training course within the Phase II time period. Manpower, Education and Training's philosophy is that the more complete "vocational" training courses are largely wasted since employers generally retrain new employees to do specific jobs. Therefore, Manpower, Education and Training supplies only the basics in its three areas of training and assumes that the employer will continue the employee's training after job placement.

Wives do not generally participate in prevocational training programs. They are provided foundation education on a half-time basis if they wish, but they are not required to participate. Some wives spend half of their time working in the Child Development Center or in the program's medical facility. They receive the minimum wage for this work and are considered to have received prevocational training as a child care aide or nurse's aide. Some wives have later been placed in jobs as a result of this experience.

The residential center can accommodate up to 40 families. Families are housed in trailers. The residential center has three permanent buildings, a recreational facility, a building housing the child development center, the medical facility, and the Phase II administrative offices, and a building for the training facilities.

Phase III includes job development and placement, the move from the residential center into private housing near the job, and follow-up counseling. Manpower, Education and Training also provides assistance to its families in locating and arranging for housing. Job placements are mostly in the area around Houston, where the unemployment rate is relatively low when compared with the base area. Follow-up counseling activities include referrals to available supportive services, employer liaison to solve job-oriented problems, assistance in transferring children into schools and child-care centers, and preventive, crisis and regular periodic counseling for all family members.

Manpower, Education and Training regards the residential phase of the Total Family Relocation Program as serving a vital cultural need of its participant-families. They are all Chicano families who are being uprooted from their home base areas. Although they are used to migrating to obtain work, they always return to their home areas where there are friends, neighbors, and extended families. The residential phase of the relocation program serves as a transition from the old life to the new life. Since other Chicano families, their neighbors at the residential center, are also making this transition, the cultural shock resulting from the initial move is reduced. At the residential center, families acquire new friends who will be living nearby after all are placed in their new jobs. A family's chance of success in their new life can thus be enhanced as a result of the Phase II residential-training approach.

The residential center began operating in November 1972. In June 1973, it was destroyed by a flood. About halfway through the restoration of the center, in November 1973, another flood occurred. The center did not become operational again until late January 1974.

Migrant and Seasonal Farmworkers Association, Inc.

Migrant and Seasonal Farmworkers Association, Inc., a nonprofit North Carolina corporation, operates a family-residential training center in the small town of Rich Square, North Carolina. The training center, a federally-owned facility, is located on two sites. The first site is a five-acre tract of land with 11 administrative and classroom mobile units (trailers) and 50 mobile homes for participant-family residences. The second site, within easy walking distance of the first, is a building utilized for vocational shops, adult education classrooms, an assembly/reception area, and office cubicles for vocational instructors.

In addition to the training center, the Migrant and Seasonal Farm-workers Association operates a large number of programs for farmworkers throughout North Carolina. These include job placement and training, adult education, emergency food and medical services, family planning services, child care services, economic development projects, and rural housing services. For example, one of the more successful eco-nomic development projects is a co-op on the North Carolina coast which employs seasonal farmworkers in the offseason to manufacture crabpots and to harvest eels for marketing to European countries. All of these operations, including the training center, are administratively controlled from the Migrant and Seasonal Farmworker Association's corporate headquarters in Raleigh, North Carolina.

The training center has been in existence since 1968. The original grantee was the Choanoke Area Development Association (CADA). The program was then called the "CADA Family Development Project." RCA Corporation provided instruction and training-related administrative services under a subcontract with the grantee. These services included administration of the training-related activities of the center, instruc-tion in adult basic education, home management, and vocational train-ing, child care, counseling, and general services such as medical, recreational, job placement assistance, and so on. CADA performed all program functions related to recruitment, accounting, legal matters, and maintenance of facilities. The accounting function included the payment of stipends to participant-families.

Recruitment for the CADA Family Development Project was an out-reach function of four nonresidential auxiliary training centers, one in each of the four counties served by the Choanoke Area Development Association. The adult basic education and prevocational training offered by these centers was referred to as "Phase I" training. Adult male participants received stipends and commuted to these nonresidential centers until they achieved the level of educational ability required to enter the "Phase II" residential training program. The nonresidential phase served as a screening component for the residential phase, since most participants who could not adapt to this type of training dropped out before entering Phase II. Also, in some instances, trainees were placed in jobs after completing Phase I training.

In 1972 the CADA Family Development Project began to evolve from its original to its present form. Early in that year the nonresi-dential centers were abolished as an economy move and the North Carolina Council of Churches' Migrant Project assumed responsibility for recruitment, relocation, and placement. The recruitment and placement areas were expanded to include the entire state. Near the end of the year the North Carolina Council of Churches became the primary grantee with CADA becoming a delegate agency and the RCA Corporation continuing as a subcontractor to the CADA. In the meantime, the Migrant and Seasonal Farmworkers Association was organized and filed its articles of incorporation. After its formation, the Migrant and Seasonal Farmworkers Association assumed the role of grantee and took over the operation of the present residential training center from the RCA Corporation and CADA when the contract between the latter two expired in early 1973.

The current Migrant and Seasonal Farmworkers Association's family-residential training center serves at any one time up to 50 families in residence and operates the following program components:

- vocational training, for the male head-of-household and, if desired, the spouse
- educational training, as required by the participant's chosen vocation
- guidance and counseling
- medical services
- home management training
- child development and daycare services
- financial support

In addition to these components, the six regional offices of the Migrant and Seasonal Farmworkers Association perform the recruiting, placement, and follow-up support functions on a statewide basis. The target population for the training center includes all migrant and seasonal farmworkers' families in the state of North Carolina, estimated to be 86,440 in number. The statewide program of the Migrant and Seasonal Farmworkers Association attempts to contact every migrant and seasonal farmworker family in the state, and to provide them with necessary assistance. To the extent feasible, those who are eligible and desirous of training are referred to the training center. This process includes a visit to the center and interviews with staff members. Upon entry to the training center program, a period of orientation is commenced. This includes:

- general tour of the center and explanation of program details
- moving into new home
- provision of household necessities
- activation of services
- counseling
- vocational interest and achievement testing
- enrollment of school-age children into local schools
- enrollment of preschool children into the daycare program
- visitation of vocational courses
- final determination of and assignment to a vocational course

The vocational training component includes training in welding, electronics, auto mechanics, and plumbing and wiring for men; and in electronic component assembly, retail sales and general office, nurse's aide, and daycare aide for women. A typical training program requires from five to ten months, depending on the number of segments completed and the rate at which the trainee is able to proceed. Each segment is designed so that it qualifies those completing it for employment in the area at a given level or in a given specialization.

The number of segments within a course is derived in one of three ways. First, there are training programs, such as auto mechanics, in which a segment consists of mastery of one area of specialization. In these programs, trainees advance in competency through the accumulation of completed segments. Second, there are programs, such as electronics and welding, which require succession from one level of achievement to another, so that each segment is more difficult than its predecessor and entry into each segment requires the successful completion of lower-level segments. Third, in courses which utilize on-the-job training, the definitions of segments are flexible, allowing enrollees to acquire ability through the completion of diversified projects. Depending on the training course and segment within that course, the successful completion of a segment is determined through testing, accomplishment of a predetermined set of procedures (such as engine disassembly and assembly), or affirmation of the instructor.

After participants are enrolled in their courses, a projected date of completion is recorded, based upon the average length of the course. Forty- five days prior to this projected graduation date, the participant is called for the first of many placement conferences. These conferences are designed to ascertain the participant's choice of placement location, housing requirements, salary desires, actual job duties preferred and suitable, and any problems related to placement and relocation. Contact is made with the district placement staff in the location of the participant's choice, regarding the upcoming graduation, placement, and relocation. Details covered during the placement conferences are also transmitted to the appropriate district staff members and a comprehensive resume of the participant, for use by the district placement staff, is developed from input submitted by the personal counselor and instructors. The district staff then immediately begins to develop job and housing possibilities.

During the final 45 days, the participant also completes an intensive course in job readiness, including the interview process, the work attitude, and many other factors designed to assist him and his family in their final transition from the training center to the world of work.

When job possibilities arise which interest a participant, interviews are arranged with potential employers. At times, it is necessary for training center staff to accompany the participant, at

times for district staff to do so. The graduate is assured, however,
of being accompanied, as well as of all necessary arrangements
involving transportation, class scheduling, and interview times.
Before each interview, the training center placement counselor will
attempt to set him at ease while advising him as to appearance and
manner expected. During their final days in the program, participants
work with the district placement counselor in preparation for relocation
and the district placement counselor will oversee such things as
packing, travel arrangements, loading, and assuring that the participant has food and other necessities to last until his first payday.
Preparations are also made for special problems such as an expect-
ant wife, a recent illness, or similar situations. The move to the
new location is conducted with the assistance of a staff member. A
family is left on their own only after complete suitability of living
conditions is assured.

   After the participant and his family have been settled in their new
environment, periodic visits are made by appropriate staff located in
the district of relocation. These visits are for the purpose of assessing any further needs of the family and assuring that any new services
deemed necessary at that time are provided. For example, the family
may not be aware of the range of social services available to them,
and they may be referred to any of several agencies or organizations.

United Tribes Employment Training Center

   The United Tribes Employment Training Center (UTETC) is operated
in Bismarck, North Dakota, by the United Tribes of North Dakota
Development Corporation. This corporation was formed specifically
to manage the program and was the first Native American organization
to operate one of the BIA's employment training centers. Previously
the Center had been run by the Bendix Corporation under contract to
the BIA.

   UTETC's facilities are extraordinarily good, and well-suited for
this type of program. Old Fort Lincoln (ironically a former cavalry
post) is the program's site. These facilities are now owned by the
United Tribes of North Dakota Development Corporation, having been
ceded to the corporation by the federal government, specifically the
Department of the Army. The administrative offices and some staff
quarters are housed in what once was senior officers' housing. These
buildings are substantial brick structures with fireplaces in nearly
every room, which face a large tree-lined area which once served the
Army as a parade ground. UTETC intends to erect new training facilities
on the former parade ground. Also on the site are all of the present
training facilities; trainee quarters, including 50 houses for families;
an accredited elementary school for the trainee's children; the child
development center; auto shops; and other buildings housing various
program components.

Trainees generally spend a year at UTETC. Vocational training includes such courses as welding, auto mechanics, building trades, and counseling aide. Trainees without a high school education participate in the necessary foundation education leading to the GED (a high school equivalency diploma based on the General Education Development test). There is some training in "life skills," such as personal grooming and home management. The main objective of the program is to train Native Americans from reservations to displace non-Native-Americans to work in the service industries on these reservations, thus accomplishing the simultaneous goals of preserving cultural life on the reservation and upgrading reservation residents both economically and educationally.

Although the target population is designated to be Native Americans from all over the United States, in fact about 90 percent of the program's participants are from the Dakotas. Their dropout rate is aound 67 percent, unusually high for this type of program (although UTETC is not completely a family-residential program; only 50 out of 150 of their trainees are married with their families in residence).

UTETC's annual budget is about $1.5 million. This figure does not include stipends, which are paid for out of money committed by the trainee's home reservation and the local BIA employment assistance officer.

2

THE ARIZONA JOB
COLLEGES PROGRAM

Arizona Job Colleges is a comprehensive family rehabilitation program for rural poor families in Arizona. The program provides for its
client-family members vocational training, aid in job development and
placement, basic and vocational-related education, and a variety of
supporting services designed to enable rural disadvantaged families to
secure and retain skilled employment.

AJC attempts simultaneously to deal with the entire range of a rural
disadvantaged family's problems, in order to prepare the family to be a
more fully-functioning unit in the community. The program therefore
includes as backup for work training the following other components:
medical and child care, remedial education, tutoring, vocational interest and work evaluation, counseling, training in home management
skills and family interactions, and the development of adequate aspirations and goals for all family members. Participant-families receive
a monthly stipend for which they are expected to attend all training
sessions and official functions of the program. Low-cost but adequate
housing is arranged for each partcipant-family in a public housing project that is mostly occupied by these families. The program regards
community living as an important environmental factor in their program;
hence families are expected to participate in "family-government"
meetings and other social functions during their training.

The initial operational phase began on July 1, 1970. During this
pilot phase, ten families from the target population were enrolled in
the program and trained for positions on the staff. These positions included such jobs as maintenance, parent-child center work, counselor's
aides, clerical work, and operation of the cafeteria. The initial AJC
client-families were all housed in the ten residential trailers, which
were especially designed for this purpose. These first ten families
graduated in January 1971 and immediately began work at AJC in their
many different capacities.

The second operational phase began in February 1971 when the first "regular" client-families were admitted. The rate of new admissions to the program was between ten and fifteen families each month. Since the duration of the training program was at that time one year, this intake rate caused a gradual buildup to 107 families, which has been the maximum operation level, though the original plan called for 120. Actually enrollment declined to around 70 participant-families after the initial peak.

AJC originally directed its program to the rural poor of Pinal County, Arizona. Pinal County's economy is agricultural; hence most of the poor are seasonal farm workers. Seasonal farm work characteristically offers low pay, sporadic employment, and decreasing opportunities due to increasing automation. According to the 1970 census, there are 2660 families out of a total of 15,254 in Pinal County below the poverty level. The mean annual income for these poor families is $2,181 and their average size is 4.75 people.

Since AJC began to receive funds from the Office of Economic Opportunity's Migrant Division (later transferred to the Department of Labor) in late February 1973, all incoming families in order to qualify for migrant funds must have earned at least 50 percent of their previous year's income in agriculture.

AJC requires that its client-families have a male head-of-household who is legally married to the woman of the family. In a 1968 survey of approximately 800 Pinal County poor families, 45 percent of those surveyed met AJC's original requirements. In that same survey, the ethnic distirbution of those poor families who were eligible for the program was found to be 4 percent Indian, 22 percent Black, 18 percent White, and 56 percent Mexican-American. The survey indicated that the average income for these eligible families was $2,577 and that the average family size was five.

AJC later extended the geographic area from which it recruits participants to the entire state of Arizona. The 1970 census indicates that there were at that time 13,162 whole (that is, male-head) rural families in Arizona below the poverty line and another 3,341 such families in small towns. The mean annual income for these families was $1,978. A number of other families in urban fringe areas may also qualify for admission to AJC. The fraction of these families who derive more than 50 percent of their income from farm labor is difficult to determine, primarily because of the difficulty in defining farm labor. The census lists 13,313 workers who live in rural areas or small towns and who are employed in "agriculture, forestry, and fisheries." Some low wage earners work in agriculture-related industries such as cotton gins, canneries, and feed lots; a few of these jobs might be included in the farm labor category for purposes of defining eligibility for AJC.

AJC has received support from a variety of funding sources, including the Ford Foundation, the Office of Economic Opportunity (OEO), the U.S. Department of Labor (DOL), the U.S. Department of Health,

Education and Welfare (HEW), the U.S. Department of Housing and
Urban Development (HUD), and the Arizona state Department of Vocational Rehabilitation (DVR).

In implementing its "comprehensive treatment," "residential-
family centered," "rehabilitation" philosophy, AJC operates the following program components:

1. Vocational training. All husbands, and all wives who want it,
are offered the opportunity for vocational training; most training is
purchased from outside training sources, community colleges, private
vocational training schools, but some is provided on-site at AJC and
there is some on-the-job-training.

2. Home management. All parents are expected to participate in
some parts of the home management program; teen-agers are offered
sewing and cooking lessons on a voluntary basis.

3. Child Development Center. The program provides daycare services for children from age three months through five and one-half years;
the Child Development Center also provides a training program for adults,
mostly mothers, who wish to become daycare or Head Start aides.

4. Developmental education. All adults who do not have a high
school diploma are expected to participate in the developmental education program. This program is completely individualized by means of
self-study programmed materials and is set up to provide training in
adult basic education (elementary) through preparation for the GED;
ESL (English as a second language) is also provided. The Developmental Educational program also provides tutorials for adults and
schoolage children who may need extra help.

5. Housing. AJC provides 70 two-, three-, and four-bedroom dwelling units for its participant families, in a nearby low-cost public housing project; the program also maintains ten residential three-bedroom,
two-bath trailers as dwelling units for participant-families.

6. Counseling. All families are seen at least once a month by their
counselor, since it is the counseling department's responsibility to
provide case coordination for the family, thus assuring delivery of all
applicable services to each family member.

7. Special Services. This component organizes and implements the
recreational program provided for the families and is also responsible
for establishing a teen program and activities for school-age children
for after-school hours and during the summer.

8. Medical Services. AJC's in-house medical services program
provides full medical and some dental care to all client-family members,
including hospitalization and surgery.

In addition to the various program offerings, AJC provides a number
of other services, such as testing and vocational evaluations, covering
psychological, aptitude and academic areas; stipends; job development
and placement; move-in and move-out services, including locating

housing for completers; furnishings and household equipment while in the program; and follow-up counseling and placement services for approximately one year after graduation.

Two other program components related to the admissions process are recruitment, whose function is to provide information to the target population on what AJC has to offer, arrange for entrance interviews, and so on; and screening, which assures that incoming families conform demographically to the poverty guidelines and program requirements (for instance, that they be legally married).

Certain innovative features of the AJC program are worth pointing out. AJC's original concept was devoted to the ameliorization of rural poverty, not by accepting rural-to-urban migration as a fact of life and operating a training and resettling program as to a greater or lesser extent all the other programs described above do, but rather by structuring a program which would retrain the rural poor for jobs in their home area. Thus, it was hoped that the rural poor could be helped without having to undergo the disruption of rural-to-urban migration. This philosophy led to an organizational problem; due to the limited number of poor families living in a small geographic area (and the limited number of jobs available), a training program would quickly exhaust the pool of available clients and jobs if it maintained a local focus. AJC's solution was to make the program mobile, unlike the other programs described above which import trainee families over considerable distances. Consequently, the key program operations were housed in mobile homes and the plan was that once AJC had done what it could for rural poverty in one area, it would pack up its house trailers and move the program to another area of the state. The official name of the project reported on here reflects this philosophy. In the Arizona Job Colleges, Pinal County Project, the plural colleges is a reference to the planned multisite location of a series of training programs moving around the state. Pinal County Project denotes the name of a particular site of the Arizona Job Colleges.

The uniqueness of AJC's local focus can be seen in comparing the service area of AJC and Mountain Plains. The six midwestern states served by Mountain Plains cover almost one-fourth the land mass of the 48 contiguous states; AJC began operations serving the western half of one county in Arizona. (We will show in later sections how this original plan of AJC's was done in by bureaucratic pressures.)

Another outstanding innovation of AJC's plan for a mobile job college concerned its physical facilities. As was mentioned above, mobile homes made up a nucleus of a job college which could be moved from location to location. AJC's second major innovation was to use for the rest of its facilities buildings which could be left behind when the job college left a location. To this end, AJC was instrumental in securing federal funds for a 300-unit low-income housing project and for a community center, with the understanding that it would use the community center for some of its training facilities and that then, when

it moved on to its next location, the original community would be left
with a housing project and community center.

AJC's goals, then, were much more ambitious than merely breaking
the family poverty cycle. It also tried to stem rural-to-urban migration,
stabilize the local economy, and contribute to community development
in small rural towns.

EARLY HISTORY AND OBJECTIVES

At the same time that the Migrant Opportunity Program and interested individuals in Arizona began to develop the concept of a job
college in 1966, the Ford Foundation was looking for places in which
to sponsor programs that could bring the rural poor into the mainstream
of society. Conversations among these parties and others, including
officials of the Office of Economic Opportunity (OEO), the Arizona
Council of Churches (now the Arizona Ecumenical Council), and representatives of several state and county agencies generated enough encouragement to lead to the organization of AJC. Representatives of the
Arizona Division of Vocational Rehabilitation (DVR) were among the
first to be consulted about the idea, since the proposed project was
to be a family rehabilitation program. The recognition that rehabilitation work had to be interpreted to include work with persons who were
vocationally handicapped as a result of educational or cultural (as
well as physical) factors enabled the organizers of AJC to plan for
support from agencies concerned with the rehabilitation of rural poor
people.

The initial objectives of the program were stated in general
terms as follows.

1. To improve the socioeconomic status of rural poor
families, as well as their ability to cope individually with an
improved status,

2. To integrate the rural poor into the larger community
through a diminution of their state of alienation from that community
and a greater sharing in its ideas, activities, values, and assets.

3. To prepare the underachieving rural poor for a more pro-
ucation, and vocational, social, and academic rehabilitation

4. To effect these ends through a comprehensive program of
interdependent projects of an innovative nature, total family education, and vocational, social, and academic rehabilitation.

By November 1967, AJC had incorporated. An application for
project funds for program development of a job college was submitted
to the Ford Foundation. AJC had formed a relationship with the
Arizona Council of Churches whereby the latter body would elect

AJC's directors and would receive funds in its behalf until AJC was able to secure its own tax-exempt status.

Exploration was made of both Pinal County and the Guadalupe area in Maricopa County as possible locations for the initial project, with Pinal County the eventual choice. Tentative selection of a site had been made at the Eleven Mile Labor Camp owned and operated by Pinal County. The Pinal County Board of Supervisors had passed the necessary resolution for the request of low-rent housing assistance from the federal government for new self-help housing at Eleven Mile Corner, and an application for a Section 23 grant was submitted to the U. S. Department of Housing and Urban Development (HUD).

The Ford Foundation announced its grant of $38,000 for program planning on May 1, 1968. Inquiry had also begun into other possible funding sources for the proposed program, both by the principals involved and by a consultant whose services were assigned to AJC for a period by the Ford Foundation. Explorations into possible kinds of cooperation between AJC and DVR resulted in a contract between the two groups, effective July 16, 1968. An amount of $33,000 was made available from DVR, and was matched on a 75/25 basis by $11,000 of Ford money, finance several facets of the program as a prerequisite to seeking major funding for the implementation of the program. Specifically, AJC set out to:

- conduct an area survey of the poor to determine their numbers, their potential, their desires, and their rehabilitative needs
- conduct a job survey to ascertain kinds and numbers of job openings, both currently existing and anticipated
- develop a comprehensive rehabilitation program for entire families, which would meet their vocational, academic, health, recreational, and social needs
- locate a site for residences and a neighborhood facility for the operation of the ultimate program and develop preliminary plans for them
- develop staff requirements for the program
- locate potential funding sources for the ultimate program, both public and private, and write grant requests for submission to those sources
- develop specific, substantively detailed elements of the program
- establish relations with the community, the businesses, the college, and the public in general
- develop a detailed system of cost accounting, on the basis of which a budget could be developed for the ultimate program

Having gotten off the ground, AJC leased offices in Phoenix, and its doors officially opened on July 16, 1968.

Original Program Concepts

In recognition of the fact that poverty is a social as well as an economic problem, AJC's program was designed as a comprehensive service delivery system, combining many kinds of program elements, both existing and innovative. To the extent that program components were available through other agencies, the resources of those agencies were to be mobilized for the benefit of AJC clients. The program plan included the restructuring of environmental conditions, vocational assessment, physical restoration and health services, behavior modification and social adjustment, and general educational opportunities, as well as job skill training geared to the individual's capacities and abilities.

Ten families were to be brought into the program in the development stage to work with the staff in identifying needs in terms of jobs, family stability, and housing. These ten were to receive the services identified above, but were also to be specially trained to become permanent staff of the job college. It was hoped that the wives as well as the husbands in these families would assume positions in the long-run operation of the program.

Following this phase of the program, 100 families were to become involved, consisting of 200 adults and approximately 370 children. Following a gradual phase-in, full operating capacity would continue at 100 families, and this number was to be maintained by the entrance of new enrollees as the original families graduated and departed. Programs would be individualized for clients in such a way that graduation and entry into the community job market would take place on a continuous-flow basis.

The cooperative interagency approach to the solution of these problems involved, in addition to the Arizona DVR, the Ford Foundation, the Arizona Department of Public Welfare, the Arizona State Employment Service, the U. S. Public Health Service, the Department of Vocational Education, and HUD. Each agency provided a vital part of the program.

1. Recruitment. Client-participants were to be recruited from the project target area through referrals from the community at large, from participating agencies, from the initial survey groups, and other sources; the screening process was based on criteria in keeping with the eligibility guidelines of DVR and the Department of Public Welfare (later done on OEO guidelines).

2. Relocation. When eligibility has been established and the client accepted into the AJC program, the family was to be relocated into low-rent housing provided for participants in the AJC program through a HUD grant.

3. Maintenance. During the rehabilitation period, living needs were to be met either through supplemental maintenance funds from the DVR or from other grant funds.

4. Vocational evaluation. In AJC's original plan, each client was to receive full physical, vocational, and psychological evaluation, not only in order to determine eligibility for this program, but also to give direction in program and curriculum planning. This evaluation was to include a full work sample evaluation. Services to the members of the client's family were to be provided when they would contribute substantially to the rehabilitation of the family head.

5. Program and curriculum planning. The industrial development and placement specialists were to locate and develop job categories and job openings with local industry to which clients could be matched as their program and curriculum were being initially planned. Each client was to be provided necessary academic remediation through adult basic education classes, as well as full vocational and skill training in the predetermined employment area. The wife of each client was to receive special adult basic education training, as well as specific training in family living, home management, child development, home economics, and other matters relative to the social adjustment and attitudinal modifications necessary for full participation in the life of the community. Educational and vocational classes were to be contracted with existing available sources when possible; if, however, they were not available, or not in keeping with the needs and objectives of AJC, classes in specific areas of interest would be established by AJC itself.

6. Full family involvement. The AJC objective of providing total programming for the entire family recognized that the support and encouragement of a client's family are essential to his success. Under the plan, preschool and school-age members of the client-family also benefit from this comprehensive program. Since both father and mother of the client family would be engaged in fulltime training or educational programs, preschool children were to be cared for in a child care center located within walking distance of client-family housing. Special programs of an educational nature were to be carried on as a regular part of the child care schedule. School-age children would attend classes in the public school system of the host community. Specific programs were to be designed in cooperation with the school system to facilitate the involvement of client-children in the mainstream of public school functions and society. In addition to this, both recreational and avocational programs and activities

were to be scheduled in the AJC program, and a teen room and
general recreation facilities were to be at the disposal of these
school children on a regular basis; tutorial services were to be
made available as needed.

7. Medical program. The medical program of AJC was conceived of as composed of several facets. Where clients had
indentifiable and specific physical disabilities which would
interfere with productive employment, DVR was to provide whatever
services were necessary to minimize or eliminate the employment
barrier imposed by such physical limitation.

8. Counseling. The counseling service of AJC was of para-
mount importance under the plan. The counselor/client ratio was
set at fifteen families to one counselor in order to provide a most
intensive and personal counseling climate. (However, OEO changed
the ratio to 37:1 on the grounds that the 15:1 ratio was not likely to
be replicable in future programs.) Through the efforts of this program,
utilizing a variety of counseling methods and psychological approaches,
it was planned that problems of a vocational, family, or social nature
could be dealt with effectively. It was also anticipated that a certain
modification of client attitudes, particularly those relating to self-
concept and chronic failure, would be effected, not only by the client
himself, but also by other members of the family.

9. Recreation and avocation. A full and ongoing program of
recreational and avocational activities was planned for all members
of the client-family, in addition to the school-age program already
indicated. Play and game facilities, as well as a hobby shop,
were recommended for adult clients, and programs of a recreational or
instructional nature, including music, movies, panel discussions,
lectures, and demonstration fellowships, were included to enliven
and enhance the clients' participation and growth during their stay
at AJC. A program of avocational activities, such as field trips,
visits to neighboring industry and historical sites, involvement in
seminars or conferences, and programs of general interest, within
and outside the community, were intended to provide an additional
catalyst toward modification of client attitudes and improvement of
self-image in relation to the total community.

10. Placement and follow-up. Vocational training programs
were to be designed on the assumption of predetermined job clas-
sifications. Near the completion of the first period of training, the
placement specialist, in consultation with the vocational rehabilitation counselor and the industrial development specialist, was to
match job vacancies with particular client abilities, skills, and
interest. One the basis of decisions in this area, the client would
enter a work experience, or on-the-job training phase of participation.
Job placement in all cases was to be effected by the placement
department of AJC, in cooperation with DVR and other existing state

agencies, and in keeping with their policies and procedures. A systematic procedure of follow-up was planned after placement and case closure, to assist former clients to maintain themselves in employment. Counselors were to visit the clients both on the job and in their homes, to offer such guidance and assistance in their new social adjustment as might be necessary or desired. This follow-up service was meant to provide a continuing interest in the client family until adequate adjustments had been established. In preparation for graduation, each family was to be provided the necessary assistance by housing specialists in locating suitable housing near its new employment. The housing specialist was to assist the family in arranging for necessary financing, and was to arrange their move from the AJC facilities to their new home. This expense was to be borne by funds provided through grant resources.

11. Facilities . As referred to earlier, client housing was to be provided through funds granted by HUD, under the Housing Assistance Provisions of their law, a total of 300 units were granted to the Pinal County Housing Authority. Priority was to be established for enrollees of AJC. Plans were made for 105 of these units to be used for this purpose, with the others distributed among other Pinal County locations. A community facility was also planned, which would provide space for the various functions of the AJC program; the children's program was to be housed in this facility, as were the recreational and avocational programs, medical services, counseling facilities, and some training facilities for home management, health education, and tutorial services. (A more detailed description of this facility follows in a later section.) At the initial stage of operation, before construction could be completed on either the homes or the community center, the program was to be carried out in a series of trailers, which would provide both residential and program space. When they were no longer needed for these purposes, the trailers were to remain in the possession of AJC and would provide the identical core of facility space when the operation was to move to a new location to start the project in replication.

Operations Before 1970

In the first funding period, from July 16, 1968 through January 15, 1969, the details of setting up operation were accomplished, contracts were established with county and educational leaders, and the first large project was undertaken, the survey of the poor in western Pinal County. A questionnaire was designed by an AJC staff member, who also supervised and trained his staff of interviewers and reviewed their work. (The results of the survey are contained in SSS 1971.)

In November 1968, AJC staff members, accompanied by members of the DVR staff, went to San Francisco for their first meeting with regional representatives of a number of federal agencies. The trip succeeded in its purpose, which was to open the door to subsequent relations with regional offices of federal agencies, and to establish personal relationships with representatives of those agencies.

During the first funding period, plans were made to contract a large share of the planning effort to the Graflex Corporation. These plans were abandoned in favor of the purchase of consulting services from them. This consulting relationship existed for a time during the fall of 1968, and resulted in assistance in starting off the writing of the ultimate program plan, and in the budgetary structure which was used in developing the final working figures.

In December 1968, the AJC governing board agreed to request additional funds and time for the development of the rehabilitation program. This request was made of DVR, and approved for the period of January 16, 1969 through June 30, 1969.

Early in the second funding period, AJC staff made a trip to Washington to open contacts with persons at the Office of Education HUD, HEW, the Inter-Agency Commission on Mexican-American Affairs, and other agencies.

In the second funding period, a decision was made not to contract any part of the operation of AJC to any outside business organization, with the possible exception of Central Arizona College (CAC) for the academic instruction of vocational programs. It was the intention of the AJC staff that instructional services would be purchased from CAC if they fit the particular needs of AJC clients.

Location was another subject which consumed a considerable amount of time and energy. The original plan for location at Eleven Mile Corner anticipated that AJC would borrow capital for the construction of homes, with Federal Housing Administration (FHA) insurance of the loan. However, the FHA insuring office rejected the location, on the grounds that it was too far away from available community services to be a good economic risk for the future. A new application for Section 23 Leased Housing was filed by the Pinal County Housing Authority, with primary assistance from AJC. Discussions were held with civil leaders of both Coolidge and Casa Grande about the advantages of each location and the cooperation necessary to acquire a Neighborhood Facility grant from HUD. Finally, the decision was made to locate in Casa Grande because of the greater growth potential of that city.

In April 1969, a presentation of the proposed job college plan was made to the Arizona Welfare Board, which agreed unanimously to support the AJC effort by submitting to HEW, in its behalf, a request for Demonstration Funds in Public Assistance. That request, because of the groundwork which had been laid for it in the regional Social and

Rehabilitation Service (SRS) office, went through the regional to the central office of SRS with an affirmative interoffice recommendation in less than a week.

During these months (January–June 1969), grant applications were prepared and submitted for an Initial Staffing Grant and a Construction Grant for a rehabilitation facility, both of which were approved before the end of the fiscal year. The writing of a proposal for funds for a health services project was also begun, and discussions were held with many interested persons, including the state Commissioner of Health, the county Health Commissioner, the director of the state Health Planning Authority, the chairman of the Department of Commuity Medicine at the University of Arizona Medical School, and several doctors in the Maricopa County Health Department.

Discussions with representatives of HUD about the request for a neighborhood center led to the selection of a five-acre piece of land on Cottonwood Lane, Casa Grande, for the neighborhood facility. An option was purchased on the land. The placement of the facility created a conflict between the requirements of two branches of HUD. On the one hand, the neighborhood facility was required to be located where it would be accessible to a large proportion of the low- and middle-income families in the area. On the other hand, the office responsible for the rent supplements for the residents would not permit the new housing to be constructed in an already-depressed area. However, because both offices were so favorably inclined toward the project and anxious to make it go, it was possible to compromise between these requirements at the Cottonwood Lane location, because of the presence of low-income families not far away.

On the east side of Pinal Avenue, however, there were a few home-owners who felt that the presence of the job college in their part of town would lower their property values. Since it appeared that some of their opposition was based on ignorance of the facts, several talks were given to civic groups to explain the program, and AJC staff members were invited to an open meeting sponsored by the City Council for the purpose of answering questions. Much of the apprehension seemed to be allayed by a more thorough understanding. Nonetheless, a lawsuit was filed by a Casa Grande resident to prevent the city from making application for a neighborhood facility to be used primarily by AJC under Section 703 of the Housing and Urban Development Act.

Three months of litigation followed, until the matter was resolved in favor of the job college. Much valuable time and energy were lost to this diversion. During that period of litigation, Mr. John P. Frank of Phoenix volunteered his services as Special Counsel for the City of Casa Grande.

In June, AJC requested additional funds from DVR to complete the development of the program and received a final extension to October 15, 1969.

For what was intended to be the implementation period, four additional staff members were added, a bookkeeper and specialists in industrial development, program development, and intercultural relations.

A major activity during the third operating period (July 1 - October
15, 1969) was the narrowing down of possibilities for the first ten families, and a preliminary screening of candidates for those positions.

In August 1969, the Ford Foundation approved a grant of $887,834
to AJC, to provide "partial support for a demonstration program in comprehensive rehabilitation and retraining of migrant farm labor." Since
the funds were to provide the matching share for federal grants, release
of the Ford funds was conditional upon authorization of the necessary
federal grants.

In August, a letter of intent was sent to VISTA indicating an interest in having a number of volunteers assigned to the project.

Members of the AJC staff made another trip to Washington in early
September, in an effort to expedite the award of the welfare grant. They
also met with the acting deputy director of OEO, who was interested in
the proposed project and invited them to submit a proposal as an alternative to the welfare proposal. It was submitted before the end of
September; also submitted at the same time was a proposal for a minority internship training program.

As the end of the third funding period approached, funding prospects were no better than they had been several months earlier, primarily because of the delay of Congress in passing the necessary appropriations bills. A decision was made to request no further funds to
cover the wait for the necessary decisions, but instead to request permission from both the Ford Foundation and DVR to use up remaining
funds beyond the specified time period. As the months had proceeded
without action, certain activities had been curtailed and expenses held
down, so that there were some funds that would be unexpended by
October 15. Permission was granted, and plans were made for the last
waiting period.

From October 15, 1969 to March 1970, the staff went on an economy
basis. While program development continued, expenditures were reduced wherever possible. Some leased equipment was returned, mile-
age compensation was cut in half, and the staff indicated a willingness
to operate at whatever personal costs to themselves that might be
necessary in order to wait out the period until the appropriations came
through. By December 1, the situation on funding was as follows:

● the Neighborhood Facility grant was approved in the amount of $564,
  000, and the architect was preparing working drawings

● a small grant of $6,300 had been committed by the Adult Education
  Division of the State Department of Public Instruction, and a proposal had been submitted to the U.S. Office of Education for a
  three year operation of a community mobile learning center

- the Section 1115 welfare grant was awaiting the Congressional appropriation before any further consideration would be given be given

- the OEO proposal was awaiting not only Congressional appropriations but authorization as well (the agency had been operating without any legal authority since the end of the preceding fiscal year)

- the grant for the purchase of trailers was approved, and action was waiting only for matching funds to be released

- the staffing grant was secure, with funds already in a Phoenix bank. But use was contingent upon securing the release of Ford funds

It was agreed among the staff and the Board that only a holding operation could continue, although the receipt of either of the two possible operating grants would enable the Job Colleges to move into full operation in approximately one month's time. The entire staff went on half-pay beginning November 30, and then went on leave without pay as of December 15. The expenditure of funds was permitted only for such necessities as rent, telephone, furniture leasing, tax obligations, and other necessary incident expenses.

The announcement in March 1970 that OEO would fund its program enabled AJC to obtain release of their Ford Foundation funds. Release of the Ford money allowed, in turn, the use of the two Rehabilitative Services Administration (RSA) grants. Hence, AJC was able to resume operations and begin purchasing facilities.

In March 1970, the Cottonwood Mobile Park was chosen as the AJC site and a lease was executed. At the same time, the AJC business manager was hired. In April staff members began to move to Casa Grande and the first trailer was delivered to the AJC site there. The next month saw the first client-family admitted to AJC and the addition of the family services manager to the staff.

In June 1970, the orientation of the first ten pilot families began. The Pinal County project of AJC became operational with the placement of trailers and installation of equipment. The instructional manager, property control supervisor, and home living supervisor were brought on board at that time. The next month saw the completion of trailer deliveries to the Casa Grande site. The home living center became operational at that time. In August, the entire AJC mobile complex became operational. The Phoenix office of AJC was closed; and AJC was formally dedicated on September 16, 1970.

On January 31, 1971, the first ten families were graduated from AJC, and the next month, 17 of the adults of those families went on the AJC payroll. Also in February, the first 20 regular client-families were admitted to AJC, and a warehouse and tutorial facility across from the trailer facility was rented. In March 1971, seven VISTA

volunteers began work at AJC. Admissions to AJC have continued at a
rate of approximately 10-15 new families per month. Since the training
program is approximately one year, this intake rate caused a gradual
buildup to 107 families, which was the maximum AJC has ever operated
with, though the original plan called for 120. Actually, AJC has had
an average enrollment of approximately 70 families over the past six
months and intends to average approximately 80 in the future.

EVALUATION RESEARCH

OEO became involved with AJC through its Office of Program Development, one of its major social research and demonstration program
operating offices. Since OEO viewed AJC as an opportunity to demon-
strate the effectiveness of some innovative program concepts in family
rehabilitation, OEO began planning an evaluation study of AJC. In 1970,
OEO contracted with the firm of Systems, Science, and Software of La
Jolla, California to conduct the evaluation. After AJC was transferred
to the Department of Labor, the evaluation was completed by the firm
of Policy Development Consultants of La Jolla, California.

In keeping with the AJC philosophy, the primary concern of the
evaluation was to determine whether attendance at AJC leads to improvement in several areas of the client-families' life, specifically in their
jobs and incomes, family activities, community activities, material
well-being, consumer practices, and attitudes and outlook on life.

The major component of the evaluation was a series of interviews
with the client-families designed to determine at several points in time
their status on those aspects of family lifestyle with which AJC was
concerned (see SSS 1971 for details of the evaluation plan). Interviews
were conducted at four times: during the first week of attendance at
AJC (entry interview); during the family's last week of attendance at
AJC (exit interview); four months after leaving AJC; and eight months
after leaving AJC. The entry interview provided the baseline—it told
where the families were before enrolling in AJC. The exit interview
told what happened to the families during their year at AJC, and the
follow-up interviews, when compared to the entry interview, were
used to determine what difference going to AJC made in the families'
lives. The interviews were administered to both parents of the first
105 families to enter AJC's regular program operation. The first part
of the interview was given to the husband and wife together in order
to collect overall family information—demographic data, family income,
property ownership, description of home and furnishings, and so on.
The second part of the interview was administered separately to the
husband and wife to collect data on their individual job history; their
attitudes toward work, self, family, and community; their alienation;
their family activities; and their social activities in the community.

A number of other data sources were also used for the evaluation. Throughout the three years of the study, the evaluation staff made periodic visits to AJC to observe the program's operation and progress. These observations provided the base for a qualitative (case history) analysis of AJC's operations. To help track the organizational growth of AJC, the Litwin Organizational Climate Index was administered to the AJC staff three times at approximately six-month intervals. Data on AJC's funding sources and pattern of expenditures was collected and a financial analysis was performed.

In 1968, before beginning its operations, AJC conducted a survey of the Pinal County poor. In April 1973, the evaluation team reinterviewed a subsample of the AJC survey sample in order to estimate what economic change, if any, would have taken place among AJC's client population of the absence of AJC.

THE FIRST TEN FAMILIES

An interesting and highly successful innovation of AJC's program was the six-month pilot phase involving ten families which provided a shakedown of the AJC operation and trained indigenous staff. These ten families moved into house trailers located at AJC, and 20 adults (both parents from each family) began training in June and July of 1970. The evaluation team interviewed the pilot families in January and June of 1971 to pre-test interview instruments and to evaluate the pilot phase.

The criterion used by AJC to select client-families for the pilot phase differed from those used in AJC's operational phase in that pilot families were more intensively screened for their motivation to participate in the program and to achieve change; for good work records; for willingness to participate in the pilot program; and, for the men, for agreement to consider post-training employment at AJC. None of the women were required to make a commitment to working (at AJC or elsewhere) as an entry criterion; however, all ten were employed at AJC after graduation. In the exit interview, one woman who had previous training as a sewing machine operator said that she had not wanted vocational training when she entered AJC because she had no desire to seek employment. In reply to our question, "What made you change your mind?" she said that everyone in the training program seemed to be having such a good time that she decided she couldn't resist. She became an aide very highly rated by her supervisor.

During the six-month pilot phase training period from June 1970 to January 1971, nine of the ten eligible members of the pilot group earned GED's (a high school equivalency diploma) and several trainees enrolled in courses at the local community college.

In January 1971, 19 of the 20 pilot enrollees completed training
and, at the time of the follow-up interview six months later, all
were employed, with 18 working at AJC in the following jobs:

Occupation	Number
Counselor's Aide	3
Instructor's Aide	2
Parent/Child Center Aide	3
Home Living Aide	3
Accounting Clerk	1
Maintenance Man	2
Storesman	1
Driver	1
Property Control Clerk	1
Receptionist	1
Total	18

AJC attributes the program's success in training and employing
the wives as well as the husbands to the fact that AJC made a point
of showing the families the advantages of two incomes over one.
Family size and age of the children were not related to employment
among the wives.

The data gathered from the pilot group were primarily economic.
No attempt was made to measure personal and social integration with
these families (there was one marriage separation since graduation).
Among the economic indicators the most striking difference, (which
was, of course, expected) was in annual income. The average increase was $5,150 per year. The decrease in average number of
persons in each room in the clients' homes was 0.412. Average
yearly food expenditures increased by $273, and clothing expenditures
by $177. (These figures denote a change in pre- and post-means
significant beyond the .05 level, in a two-tailed t-test.) The accuracy
of the clothing estimate is probably not very high. The annual rate
was based on expenditures in the five months previous to the interview, and during that time the families probably bought more clothes
than usual, because they needed to "catch up" in their wardrobes.
The average decrease in indebtedness was $542 (not statistically
significant).

One of the most persistent and difficult problems among the
families at AJC has been excessive indebtedness. In our early
interviews with AJC administrative personnel, we were told that
budgeting with families so they could live on their stipends was
greatly complicated by their other (sometimes unreported) financial
obligations. AJC staff members were obliged to do "debt counseling,"

as well as to intercede with bill collectors, who often harassed
the client-families. The question of a policy on bankruptcy came up
in the first month of the pilot phase because one family of this
group was so deeply in debt. That family later went through bankruptcy, though AJC's policy was to avoid it if at all possible.

Of the ten families in the pilot group, nine said they had paid
interest at some time prior to January 27, 1971. In six of these
families, at least one spouse could explain what interest was. Only
two people from different families knew how much interest they were
paying, or had paid, before enrolling in AJC.

In response to the question, "What did you think you would be
doing during the course of your training at AJC?" five of the nineteen
said they expected to get the training (vocational) that they got;
three said they had expected different training, and had been dis-
appointed but were now satisfied; two said they had expected more
than they got, but only one expressed disappointment; the others
named some single aspect of the program which they did receive
(such as more education or work with children) as their expectation.

In response to the question, "What changes in your life did you
expect as a result of your training at AJC?" fourteen said they expected
a higher income and a better job, either for themself or their spouse;
ten said they expected to have a better home and/or family life. The
rest expressed individual expectations for more education, more
community participation, better chances for children, and so on.

Upon graduation, twelve of the nineteen were registered to vote;
of the seven not registered, four at that time were below the voting age.

Of the 18 who replied, 16 mentioned that they now budget, plan,
save more, and are more price-conscious or make a list when shopping,
as a result of their training at AJC. Another said that she now provides
better food for her family; only one said he had made no changes in
his buying habits.

PILOT PHASE: CONCLUSIONS

The six and one-half month pilot phase was, in our judgment,
an extremely good investment for AJC. In addition to allowing time
for startup of program development, staff recruitment, and the construction of facilities, it produced 18 entry-level AJC staff members
who had recent experience as members of the target population. All
ten families have succeeded in improving their own socioeconomic
conditions and later actively participated in helping others. As
staff members, they are in a unique position, both as exemplars to
new families, and as intermediaries between families and regular
staff.

In addition, the pilot group demonstrated the advantages of living together, as well as learning together, during their training period, since they had the opportunity to live in the ten on-site residential trailers while in the program. As mentioned elsewhere in this study, the people themselves were aware of the positive impact of their living close together. They reported that it contributed to their feeling of a sense of community. It tended to promote their sense of identity with the AJC program, and it enhanced the impact of the program, because their proximity to each other offered opportunities for learning and practicing new problem-solving techniques in the full range of life situations on a day-to-day basis.

These 18 staff members also appear to be the nucleus of what should properly become a force for change in the larger community, as voters, as consumers, as participants in local affairs, and as highly-motivated workers in helping others to change.

RECRUITMENT

The Recruitment department has the responsibility for locating
and helping to qualify for admission enough families to fulfill AJC's
monthly intake quotas. These intake quotas vary from month to
month, depending on graduations and terminations. Quotas are set
so as to maintain AJC's number of residential families at between
70 and 80.

Admission Requirements. AJC's entry criteria included the following
requirements: family income had to be below the Office of Economic
Opportunity (OEO) Poverty Guidelines (in 1974 the poverty limit
was $3,450 for a family of three and ranged up to $6,200 for a
family of seven); interviews with the Arizona Department of Vocational
Rehabilitation (DVR) had to be completed; AJC's testing program had
to be completed; the family had to complete a medical examination
provided by AJC. During most of its early history, AJC also required
the family heads to be legally married. Single-parent families were
not accepted into the program, but if a marriage dissolved while the
partners were in attendance at AJC, both partners were allowed to
complete their training. According to the entry criteria, a family
could be denied admission not only for earning too much money, but
also for earning it from the wrong (nonfarm) source (it should be
noted that the requirement restricting income from nonfarm sources
was not in effect at the time the families studied in this report were
admitted to AJC). Families could also be denied admission if there
were debilitating medical problems beyond the resources of AJC's
medical program or if their debt burden would be unmanagable on the
AJC stipend. The entry criteria underwent constant review and
modification, both in response to the demands of the various agencies
funding the AJC program and as a result of changes in the AJC
philosophy.

At the time of writing, AJC's admission requirements had been modified so that AJC would qualify for grant funds from the DOL Migrant Division. In order to be eligible for AJC, families must be below OEO's poverty line and must have derived at least 50 percent of their most recent year's income from farm labor.

AJC's original target population was the "rural poor in western Pinal County." AJC's original OEO grant required AJC families to be below the poverty line. Since western Pinal County is a rural area with an agricultural economy, there would be considerable overlap between the "rural poor" and migrant and seasonal farm workers (AJC's later target population). However, in the 105-family study group(see above, Chapter 2), of the 77 husbands who identified their vocations prior to entering AJC, only 41 (53 percent) had worked primarily in farm work. Thus, the change in admission requirements established by the DOL migrant grant will later alter the population from which AJC recruiters draw their families. The more restrictive admission requirements have, no doubt, contributed to the assertion by AJC's recruiters that western Pinal County is "drying up" as a source of AJC families.

Geographic Service Area and Referral Sources. AJC has expanded the geographic area served from (originally) "western Pinal County" to (at the time of writing), the entire state of Arizona. This expansion is due partly to the greater effort required to recruit from the local target population (see above) and partly to certain changes in the Arizona state government. Of particular note is the creation of the Department of Economic Security (DES), a new state superagency. DES includes the former state Department of Vocational Rehabilitation (DVR), with which AJC has had a long and mutually beneficial relationship.

DES has become a major source of referrals to AJC. These referrals occur from the six district offices of DES, and are facilitated through communications between the District Five manager (District Five includes Casa Grande), an enthusiastic supporter of AJC, and the remaining five district managers. Also, AJC's president has done an excellent job of public relations within the DES hierarchy. As a result of this work, the statewide recruiting efforts by DES in AJC's behalf receives tacit approval at the state level.

For historical interest, the sources of referrals for the 105 families in the study sample are given below.

Source of Referral	Number of Families
Word of mouth	26
AJC families	21
As a result of 1968 survey	2

Source of Referral	Number of Families
AJC staff members*	25
Referred by a local social service agency (such as Community Action Program [CAP] or Migrant Opportunity Program [MOP])	16
Walk-in	4
Not stated on application	11

Recruitment Personnel Activities. The recruitment staff consists of two recruiters under a Recruitment and JDP supervisor. The recruiter's duties include both field and on-site interviewing with potential applicants, providing assistance in meeting the requirements for documents and verification of income and employment, and setting up appointments and assisting with transportation for testing, medical examinations, and interviewing.

A family's initial contact with AJC is usually made by referral, either from another agency (DES, Churches, the Federal Bureau of Indian Affairs [BIA], MOP, schools) or from individuals who have been in or are associated with the program. Recruiters also estimate that about 25 percent of their contacts are self-referrals, (or "walk-ins" as AJC refers to them). There have been a few occasions when AJC recruiters went into certain poverty areas and rang doorbells (for example, in Stanfield and Maricopa), primarily because they were not getting people from those areas. These efforts were rated very successful by the Recruitment Department.

Whether the initial contact is made at AJC or in the field, the recruiter's first step is to make an appointment to visit with the whole family at home, so that the AJC program can be fully explained to all family members at one time and questions can be answered. The recruiters use a slide presentation as their primary tool for telling the AJC story; an excellent brochure which has been produced in both Spanish and English is left with the family.

At the time of the full family interview, after the recruiter has determined that the family is interested and at least nominally eligible (that is, appears to fall below the poverty line, derives most ot its income from farm labor, and is a whole family) a family information sheet is filled out and explained so that when the formal application is made the necessary documents can be presented. In some cases the application is taken then and there, but more often the family makes an appointment to come to AJC to visit and to fill

---

*Most of these referrals were from those AJC staff members who were themselves AJC graduates.

out the application. If documents such as birth certificates and
marriage certificates are unavailable from the family, the recruiter
takes the necessary information and sends for them. In the case
of missing W-2s or employment verification, local employers are
called. AJC recruiters also now submit the names of all applicant-
families to the welfare department to see if they are or have been
on welfare, as under the new grants former welfare clients may be
eligible for additional money.

If, after filling out the application, the family qualifies for
AJC, the adults are given appointments for physical examinations,
and begin the testing and evaluation procedures.

During this period, the recruiters often have to provide
transportation to and from AJC so that the families can keep
appointments. The travel time provides additional opportunities for
the recruiters and the families to get to know each other and provides
moral support to those who find the testing and medical procedures
difficult to deal with. This set of procedures constitutes a
preorientation period during which the adults in the families spend
many hours on-site at AJC.

When the testing and medical procedures are completed, the
families are brought up for consideration by the Acceptance Committee.
After the results of this consideration are known, the recruiters have
the responsibility for conveying and explaining the committee's
decisions to the families. If the family is accepted or deferred, the
recruiter's responsibility continues; with accepted families, the
recruiter helps to make arrangements for entry into AJC (reregistering
children in school, arranging to move, and so on), and with deferred
families the recruiter can often assist in qualifying the family for
later acceptance. Families "not accepted" are theoretically referred
elsewhere, but according to the recruiters, there is often nowhere for
many of them to get help. This has been one of the most difficult
parts of the recruitment staff's job.

AJC's recruitment staff has recently been made a part of the
"team approach" described in the section below on counseling. The
increased sense of participation provided by being thus included,
together with attendance at Acceptance Committee meetings, has
helped to overcome the feeling, expressed by some of the recruiters
in the past, of working in a bureaucratic vacuum. This feeling came
from having to do a great deal of contact and subsequent paperwork
on families of whom more than 50 percent were not accepted or
deferred. The recruiters have complained about feeling that they were
expected to mislead families by encouraging them to go through the
complicated and time-consuming application and preorientation
processes when so many of them were ultimately turned down.
Attendance at the Acceptance Committee meetings has helped to
alleviate both the recruiter's and the applicant client-families'
problems by giving the recruiter more perspective on the reasons for
selection and how these criteria are brought to bear in practice.

SCREENING AND THE ACCEPTANCE COMMITTEE

The Screening Process. After the AJC recruiters have elicited a
completed application form from a potential AJC family, the
screening process begins. The steps in the screen process are:

- verification that the family is eligible for AJC, that is,
  that the minimum admission requirements (below
  poverty line, over 50 percent of income from
  farm labor, and legal marriage) are satisfied
- a general medical exam
- an interview with a DVR counselor
- psychological tests in order to appraise the
  potentials and aptitudes of the adults in the
  family
- acceptance, deferral, or rejection by the Acceptance
  Committee (formerly called the "Selection Committee"),
  and (usually) referral of nonaccepted families to
  some other social service agency

The screening process at AJC has always sought to balance two
opposing objectives, first to keep the number of families at AJC as
close to the normal operating level (currently 80) as possible, and
second to keep the dropout rate at a minimum. During AJC's initial
buildup to full size (from early 1971 to mid-1972) there was
considerable pressure (by AJC management and from the primary
funding agency, OEO) for the screening process to stress the first
of these objectives. Hence, admission requirements were relaxed
during that period. Once full strength was achieved, the dropout
level (which reached approximately 35 percent by mid-1972 and
has persistently remained above that since) caused the second
objective to assume some importance.

Until mid-1972, an acceptance meeting was held approximately
once a month with one counselor, the instructional manager, a
psychometrist, and a member of the administration in attendance.
The proceedings were informal, and decisions about families' acceptance or nonacceptance were usually consensual. The need to
balance the two objectives listed above caused the process to become
a more demanding task. So a new procedure was initiated in the hope
that more accurate choices could be made in terms of retention and
ultimate success in the program. The kernel of this new procedure
was the Acceptance Committee, described immediately below.

The Acceptance Committee. The Acceptance Committee meets
regularly (once a month up to April 1973, and more frequently since)
to go over the case briefs on applicant-families and decide on those
that will be accepted into the AJC program. The voting members of

the Committee are all division managers (the Family Services
manager, who is chairman of the Committee, the instructional
manager, the Health Services manager, the business manager,
and the Special Services manager), a DVR counselor, and a member
of the administration. The nonvoting members are a representative
from the work evaluation section (usually a psychometrist), a
representative from the Medical Services unit, and others at the
discretion of the chairman. In the sessions observed by the research
team, the supervisor of recruitment was also present, and we were
also told that a representative from the Job Development and
Placement unit is usually included for the purpose of informing the
Committee on the job prospects for the applicant-family's preferred
vocational training field. No fewer than all seven voting members
constitute a quorum. The Committee can make any of three decisions
about each family: acceptance, nonacceptance (with or without
referral), or deferment (with or without referral). Deferment is
recommended when full information is not yet available; when
temporary, critical medical conditions pertain or when, in the judgment of the Committee, alternative interim services would be more
appropriate (referral).

In the sessions observed by the research team late in 1972, the
proceedings were as follows. The psychometrist presented test results
first, then the representative (the physician in this case) from
Medical Services discussed the parents' health, and the DVR counselor
presented the status of the family's eligibility for DVR services
within the AJC program. DVR's qualifying a family as "disabled/
disadvantaged" is important for participation in AJC because DVR
pays for many of AJC's services for DVR-eligible clients. Thus,
every effort is made to so qualify all applicant families. The other
criteria for selection are as follows: income must fall below the
poverty level, (and DOL has recently reemphasized that benefits
are not available for "upgrading," meaning that a person whose
income is above the poverty level, for whatever reason (even if he
had to work 80 hours a week) is not eligible;[*] at least 50 percent of
a family's previous year's income has to have been earned in
agricultural work; and the family must be "whole" (the man and
woman legally married, with or without children), must hold American
citizenship, and must have the motivation to change. This last factor

----

[*]Until recent months, AJC has, evidently through a misunder-
standing, prorated income on the basis of a 40-hour week, so that
some families above the poverty level in gross income were
admitted to the program (14 out of the 105 in the study sample).

is determined through interviews with the family and through personality tests administered by AJC psychometrists. By the time the committee meets, most of these criteria have already been determined.

The decision to accept or reject a family was heavily influenced by the opinion of the physician. He has the responsibility for diagnosing illnesses and then, together with the Medical Services manager, presenting a prognosis for remediation, both on medical grounds and in terms of the treatment and facilities available through the AJC medical grant. An influential factor in his recommendations was the current status of the medical grant funds, that is, whether there was more money available in the pilot group fund (AJC families) or in the control group fund (other migrant poor). In the cases where applicants had serious presenting symptoms, eligibility for BIA and/or veterans benefits was considered in justifying nonacceptance or deferment.

In light of some of AJC's early experience with families whose medical problems interfered with the training program, the caution shown in selecting against people with medical problems was no doubt justified. However, certain medical diagnoses were made that were conjectural, even to the amateur observer. For example, more than one wife was diagnosed as being a "possible syphillis" or "possible gonorrhea" case, while no mention was made of the husband's "possible" venereal condition. More than one applicant was faulted by the physician for unwillingness to go through the physical examination. This resistance was presented as evidence having some bearing on the acceptability of the family for AJC participation. Dental problems were also treated as a negative factor since AJC could, at the time, only provide "emergency" dental care. (However, dental care later became available in the AJC Medical department through the National Health Service Corps Program).

The psychometrist's evaluations, on the other hand, appeared to have weight only if there were some very negative evidence. The members of the Acceptance Committee showed a great interest in I.Q. measures, although the relevance of the information was not readily discernable. Results of the other tests were only very briefly touched upon, although the psychometrist's experience of cooperation or the lack of it with the client during testing, whenever mentioned, was treated as important. The DVR counselor's reports dealt solely with the status of the client-family with respect to eligibility for benefits.

The voting members of the Committee in most cases had had no contact with the applicants, so the recommendations of the physician, the psychometrist, and DVR were the main inputs. The recruiter's recommendations for acceptance on each application were taken for granted. The only exceptions to the above were in the cases where the recruiter had first-hand knowledge of the family and therefore made some contribution, usually one of advocacy. All in all, the decision-making process in many cases seemed arbitrary, with entirely too much importance attached to the physician's impressions. Of course, the forceful personality of the particular physician on the Committee during the period of study contributed to the Committee's deferring to his suggestions. (These observations were made in late 1972. The individual who was staff physician at that time has since died and the current physician at AJC has been described as "more people-oriented" by AJC's staff members).

Recommendations for Potential Replicated Programs. AJC recently has adopted the policy of including in the Acceptance Committee meetings at least one person (most often the recruiter) who has had personal contact with the family outside the institutional setting. The objective information of the psychometrist, the physician, and DVR is important. But subjective information on the family as a social unit and as individuals in the world is also relevant, and therefore, usually the standard phrases on the case brief do not convey any perspective on the client-families as persons. Therefore, the insights, impressions, and information of the recruiters are very useful in considering families for admission. The inclusion of the recruiters in the Acceptance Committee meetings has the added value of helping them to see more clearly the criteria for acceptance and at the same time helping them to feel more involved in AJC. The recruiter's involvement in the Acceptance Committee's procedures can probably be best facilitated by going over case briefs according to recruiter caseloads (rather than alphabetically) so that each recruiter concerned could attend the meetings for only the period of time that concerned his cases.

Early in the history of AJC, physical examinations were contracted for at a local private clinic which prepared a written report of its findings. In the authors' opinion, these written reports were superior for screening purposes to the detailed verbal reports of physical examinations usually presented in the Acceptance Committee meetings. If AJC's medical department provided written medical reports to the Acceptance Committee with a recommendation by the physician for treatment and disposition, then the physician himself would not have to come to these meetings. This would have the advantage of freeing more time for the physician to meet his extremely heavy schedule. Since the Medical Services manager is always present at Acceptance Committee meetings, he could reply to inquiries about terminology and interpret the medical jargon when necessary.

ACJ and replicated programs should develop some guidelines on the criteria for nonacceptance on medical grounds. It seems obvious that among the poverty population standards of health are certain to be lower than among the more affluent population, so the incidence of disease and disability can be expected to be relatively high.

That was the reason medical services were included in the AJC plans
for "comprehensive family rehabilitation." It is therefore incumbent
on AJC and similar programs to deliver services to a representative
sample of the rural poor population, and to be as inclusive as possible
in accepting people with health problems. Some deliberation on which
medical conditions can and cannot be constructively dealt with would
no doubt be helpful to everyone involved in delivering services to the
client-families.

TESTING AND VOCATIONAL EVALUATION

The primary activities of this program component are first, to
perform the psychological testing portion of the screening function,
and, second, to provide vocational evaluation of client-family adults
immediately after the family has been admitted to AJC. The former,
as was mentioned above, is concerned with administering intelligence
tests, and aptitude tests to adult family members who are being
considered for admission to AJC. (The list of specific tests within
each of these catagories is contained in Appendix A). Appropriate
tests for individuals within each category are selected. This
selection depends on the literacy and English-speaking ability of the
individuals; for example, for poor readers, the Picture Interest
Inventory would be utilized rather than the strong Vocational Interest
Blank, which is used with individuals who can read at the seventh
grade level and above. The objectives of this psychological testing
are to ascertain the learning potentials of the adult family members
and to measure certain personality factors which AJC deems important
for its clients (such as, motivation to change). Psychometrists who
administer these tests to applicants attend Acceptance Committee
meetings to provide subjective as well as objective data on the
families' potential success at AJC.

The vocational evaluation is concerned with helping to plan the
adult family members' training program. In this activity, individuals'
work habits, learning abilities, and general skills are observed in
simulated work situations. Certain job-related physical abilities are
measured with a variety of dexterity tests and job-sample experiments.
Tests to detect physical limitations (such as visual problems, hearing
deficiencies, or organic brain damage) which could affect an
individual's vocational objectives are administered (see Appendix A
for a list of specific tests). Potential job situations are simulated
in order to ascertain whether individuals who state certain job
preferences are really suited for that job. For example, men who
state a preference for auto mechanics are observed as they perform
typical atuo shop tasks in AJC's simulated shop environment (do they
mind getting their hands dirty?); men who state carpentry as a
preference are observed working outside (does working outside bother
them?) in typical carpentry tasks.

The psychological testing requires one to three days, depending on the particular tests administered, the family's availability, and the individuals' aptitudes. The vocational evaluation requires up to two weeks. The testing and vocational evaluation unit processes 12 to 14 people at a time with seven staff members.

Historical Background. The testing and vocational evaluation unit is relatively new at AJC, having not been established until late 1972. At that time, AJC was awarded a contract by the state of Arizona to provide certain services to Arizona welfare recipients. One of the primary services to be provided under this contract was vocational evaluation. Since AJC had no such activity, and the lack thereof had always been regarded as a serious drawback by AJC management (and the evaluation project team), this "purchased-services" contract provided the funding opportunity to establish this unit. Space was made available in a leased warehouse and a subcontract was awarded to the University of Arizona to supply psychometrists and vocational evaluation specialists, and the Testing and Vocational Evaluation (T&VE) unit began operations in January 1973.

AJC originally transported its applicant-and client-families to the Phoenix DVR office for psychological testing and vocational evaluation. However, this arrangement was quickly found to be untenable, because AJC regarded DVR's interpretation of the tests as too subjective. AJC then entered into an agreement with the University of Arizona's College of Education Rehabilitation Unit to administer the entrance "psychs" to applicant-families. Under this agreement, the university sent a team of psychometrists to AJC, so that families did not have to be transported for testing. Unfortunately, under this new arrangement, AJC clients received no vocational evaluation except for the vocational interest tests administered to applicants.

After the installation of the T&VE unit at AJC, the old agreement for testing services with the University of Arizona Rehabilitation Unit was replaced by the subcontract for professional staffing of the AJC unit mentioned above. However, since the primary responsibility of the AJC T&VE unit was to perform vocational evaluations for the Arizona welfare recipients (nonresidential AJC "day students"), resources were not available to administer the entrance "psychs" to applicant-families for the residential program. The T&VE unit did perform work evaluations on some AJC residential students (those whose vocational futures were in doubt), but from March to December of 1973 no entrance psychological tests were administered. Psychometrists at the T&VE unit attribute the high dropout rate for residential families entering during this period to the reduced screening capability resulting from the lack of entrance "psychs."

Current Situtation. Since the state of Arizona purchased-services contract with AJC has expired, the T&VE unit is now supported from other AJC resources, and is administering all of the entrance tests and vocational evaluations for AJC residential families. Hence, it is now (since December 1973) functioning as a full-fledged component of the residential program. The subcontract with the University of Arizona has been extended to provide most of the professional staffing (three psychometrists) for the T&VE unit. Currently, one professional psychometrist, one testing aide, and two secretaries comprise the T&VE unit staff people who are on AJC's payroll on a fulltime basis.

The T&VE unit is also seeking some support from sources outside AJC. They have recently begun conducting some testing services for the Casa Grande City Schools. This operation contributes to AJC's community image and, at the same time, provides AJC additional revenue to cover T&VE unit operations.

ORIENTATION

The orientation program is designed to provide incoming students with a quick overview of AJC facilities and procedures. Currently, orientation takes only one day. Table 3.1 presents a sample schedule of orientation activities.

Historical Background. AJC's orientation procedure has undergone several changes in structure. During the period in which the 105-family sample was being admitted, orientation was scheduled to cover four days, and included the interviews which were conducted by the evaluation research field interview staff. Essentially the same activities as are shown in Table 3.1 were covered, with more time allocated for each. Since four days were not really required for orientation, there were numerous "coffee breaks" and other time-structuring activities.

In November 1971, one of the authors and his spouse spent the first day of orientation with the families as a participant-observer. The orientation began, two hours late, with a tour of the parent-child center. Since it was their first day, the tour was conducted while the children were out for their morning snack, thus avoiding having the small children being upset by seeing their parents come and go.

The next item on the agenda was a talk by the AJC administration. The tone of this session was one of stern authoritarianism, stressing such things as disciplinary actions, fines for missing scheduled events in the training program, and restraint in utilizing AJC medical facilities. The effect was to severely depress the incoming families, who were nervous about their new experiences anyway.

The administration's discussion was followed by talks by two representatives of the family government. The "establishment" flavor of their presentation caused the observer to note that the incoming families had no idea of who the speakers were or what

TABLE 3.1

Orientation of New Families

(Friday, January 11, 1974)

Time	Activity	Place
8:30 – 9:30	Meet with counselors and Family Services manager	Esperanza Conference Room
9:30 – 10:00	Coffee break; Family Government discussion	Esperanza Conference Room
10:00 – 10:45	Special Services tour	Esperanza Center complex
10:45 – 11:15	Administration welcome	Esperanza Conference Room
11:15 – 11:30	Housing explanation	Esperanza Conference Room
11:30 – 12:00	Health Services exposure	Health classroom
12:00 – 1:00	Lunch	Home or Cafeteria (75¢ a person)
1:00 – 1:30	Home Living tour	Home Living trailers
1:30 – 2:00	Evaluation unit tour	Evaluation unit
2:00 – 2:30	Business Division exposure; stipend explanation	Administration Conference Room
2:30 – 3:30	Instruction Division tour	Learning Center
3:30 – 4:30	Wrap-up session with counselors	Administration Conference Room

Source: Arizona Job Colleges schedule.

47

they were there for, even after they had finished. This was too bad, since the family government organization has the potential of easing the cultural shock endured by incoming families.

The last item of the day was a discussion by a representative of AJC's Business department. He gave a fairly straight talk on the care of federal property, including a warning that stealing it was a federal offense. He explained that AJC provides such items as furniture, linens, and drapes, but not personal disposable items such as soap and toilet paper. He made a pitch for "community spirit" with regard to housing upkeep (his exact words were "We help you, now you help us") and said AJC would furnish garden tools and vacuum cleaners, and would "issue work orders" for repairs beyond the scope of handy-man type home maintenance. He explained AJC's transportation system (which includes such things as buses for special events and training) and stressed that no AJC vehicles were to be for "personal use."

In general, families were listless, bored, and apparently depressed during most of the orientation.

Feedback from the evaluation research team, and a change in management of the Family Services section caused AJC to drastically alter its orientation procedure. The orientation process was reorganized to provide a more intensive experience in each program area for the adult family members. The primary objective of the new one-month orientation period was the formation of the training plans for each family member. It was learned early in AJC's history that most people who enter AJC need wider exposure to the kinds of work available, so an extra emphasis was placed on the "world of work and vocational exploration" during orientation. In addition, both husband and wife were scheduled for introductory class sessions in the various program areas: Home Living, Family Recreation, Health Education, and Child Development; and Family Services division provided problem-oriented group counseling for one hour each day during that first month. In addition, the instructional division made its educational assessments and prescribed the academic programs to be entered into by each person.

The establishment of AJC's own testing and evaluation unit reduced the need for the long orientation period designed around vocational selection. The "world of work" introduction was moved to the Instruc-tional division, and another change in the management of the Family Services division resulted in the current one-day form of the orientation procedure. Other factors influencing the shortening of the orientation period was concern, from the new DOL sponsors, about the length of the total training period for residential families.

Recommendations for Replicated Programs. AJC's orientation pro-cedure was at first so loosely structured that many client-families spent a lot of time just sitting around. This had serious negative consequences; people were bored and frustrated, and got a false impression of what participation in AJC was like. Negative aspects of life at AJC (such as nonattendance punishments) were stressed over positive factors, contributing to the uneasiness and depression which anyone feels when they embark on a change in their life of the magnitude of the AJC experience.

The new approach to orientation appears not only to dispel the former negative effects, but by fully utilizing the time available during the first day, to ensure that all adults (both men and women) are being exposed to all program elements. This gives both partners a better understanding of what their spouse is doing at AJC. In the past, the men had at most only peripheral contact with the Home Living and Child Development divisions, and most of the women had little or no direct contact with the Job Development division and the vocational training their husbands were involved in.

HOUSING AND MAINTENANCE

A major innovative aspect of AJC is the provision of a resident-ial housing "campus" for enrollees. Most of the AJC families come from very substandard housing and part of AJC's rehabilitation program consists of providing a guided experience in living in a home with full plumbing facilities, modern appliances, and at least a bed, if not his own room, for each family member.

A central concept in the AJC housing plan was to house all families in a single neighborhood, thereby fostering a continuous sense of community among them and enabling AJC to plan organized after-hours community activities related to its overall rehabilitative goals.

AJC's residential program utilizes about 80 dwelling units for housing its client-families. Ten of these units are residential trailers purchased by AJC with Rehabilitative Services Administration con-struction grant funds; in addition, AJC leases, from the Pinal County Housing Authority (PCHA), about 70 two-, three-, and four-bedroom dwelling units in a low-cost public "turnkey" housing development. AJC was instrumental in acquiring the HUD grant which paid for constructing this turnkey housing.

AJC housing is conveniently located for the residential families. All of the dwelling units are within a two-block radius of the Esperanza Family Center, the vocational evaluation facility, and the main trailer complex, which includes AJC's administrative offices, learning center, and medical facilities. School-age children of AJC families from kinder-garten through junior high are within five blocks of their schools.

Activities of AJC's Housing and Maintenance department include:

- scheduling specific dwelling units for use by incoming families
- preparing these units for the particular families' needs (including such activities as moving in cribs for very young children, or moving in the proper numbers of beds)

- assisting incoming families in moving from their old homes into the AJC housing
- providing representation to the Acceptance Committee meetings, so that housing availability is considered as a factor in accepting or deferring eligible families
- coordinating its activities with those of PCHA
- providing all maintenance for the 80 dwellings
- procuring housing for AJC graduate-families
- physically moving the household possessions of graduate-families from their AJC housing (or from storage) into their new homes

PCHA has certain limits on the sizes of families which can occupy units with a particular number of bedrooms. The larger families are restricted to AJC's four-bedroom units, and if no such units are available, these families' entrance to AJC must be deferred. Often AJC will place a small family in a three- or four-bedroom available unit if no two bed-room units are open, and later move the small family to make room for a larger incoming family.

In procuring housing for graduate-families, the Housing and Maintenance manager accompanies the graduate-family to their first meeting with their new landlords in order to interpret and clarify terms of leases. He also accompanies families to utility company offices in order to assist them in interpreting rules regarding deposits and other such matters. Most graduate-families want to purchase a home. Hence, the Housing and Maintenance manager assists them with the forms and procedures to apply for financial assistance from the Farmer's Home Administration. Currently, there is at least a four-month wait for processing applications, so all graduate families must rent housing for some period of time. Many AJC graduate-families have been placed in one of the 35 or so dwelling units unused by AJC in the same turnkey project that the AJC residential units are in. In procuring housing, the AJC housing manager has travelled all over Arizona, to wherever AJC's graduates are placed in jobs.

Historical Notes. In the winter of 1967-68, AJC prepared an application for a Section 23 grant from the Department of Housing and Urban Development (HUD) on behalf of PCHA, with AJC to be the developer. At that time, it was proposed to locate a housing project, along with AJC, at Eleven Mile Corner, a crossroads in the desert 11 miles east of Casa Grande and 11 miles north of Eloy. This grant request was turned down as uninsurable by the Federal Housing Administration (FHA), which considered the location undesirable because it was away from service facilities.

AJC then prepared a second grant application for 300 houses to be located in either Casa Grande or Coolidge. This grant was approved and awarded to PCHA for construction. AJC decided to locate in Casa

Grande, due to its proximity to two interstate highways and consequent convenience and growth potential. The present location in northern Casa Grande was selected over another possible site which would have required dispersing the AJC housing among existing homes. AJC had priority on use of the 105 houses to be built in Casa Grande.

Events proved that getting the housing grant was just the beginning of AJC's housing problems. Even more difficult was the problem of getting the houses built. HUD required no performance bond and imposed no penalties for nonperformance. It seems that the only motive for completing a Section 23 project would be to capitalize on the immense potential for profit designed into the program. Section 23 grants include provision for each of four "fee talents," an architect, a package coordinator, a lending institution, and a contract/builder, which are not necessarily included in the overall fee, approximately 15 percent allocated to the developer. It is no doubt a highly profitable game among developers once having received the contract to perform one or more of these services, collect the fee, and then sell the remaining project to another contractor who performs some more of the services, collects his fee, sells it again, and so on; eventually somebody buys it to actually do the construction. All this buying and selling and collecting of fees seems highly profitable, and competition to get in on the money can be fierce. This is one of the problems AJC encountered. For almost two years, several housing developers bought and sold the project, collected fees, and fought court cases over who got to buy and sell what to whom. In the meantime, no houses were built.

The first developer to show interest in the project was National Housing Industries, of Phoenix. National's plans were for something called "mini-houses." When presented to the city fathers of Casa Grande, the "mini-houses" met with a very cool reception on the grounds that they appeared to be an instant slum. Nevertheless, National submitted the plan to the HUD regional office and was turned down because the costs were too high. Inquiries to FHA, HUD, National Housing, and PCHA about the amount of money in the HUD grant, or at least the average amount of money allocated for any unit of measurement (square footage, number of rooms, and so forth) elicited the response "it's a complicated formula," and none of the informants was able even to cite what HUD considered relevant factors in it. However, the HUD lease-rates on turnkey-leased housing (which is the classification of the project in Casa Grande) were obtained, and the Phoenix FHA office quoted the total value of the Casa Grande housing under the HUD grant as approximately $1.5 million, though a spokesman for National Housing said $1.7 million.

According to an article in the Casa Grande Dispatch for November 24, 1969, National's proposed housing was too high by an average of $14 a month for each house ($17,640 a year on all 105 houses). A spokesman for National Housing was quoted as saying that the turnkey

program was "unworkable. . .this thing is just not working across
the nation" and that it was uncertain whether National could modify
its plans by the deadline for resubmission of plans of December 31,
1969.

The Leo H. Daly Company stated that if National did not resubmit
they would be extremely interested. Daly, in fact, had "already worked
up a program," and had contacted officials in Casa Grande and the
Housing Authority.

In the meantime, the architect who had designed the Esperanza
Neighborhood Facility in Casa Grande submitted plans to HUD for
the 105 houses in Casa Grande and the 40 units that were scheduled
for Florence. National Housing and a local builder were also in the
competition for the Casa Grande project during some of this time,
but both dropped out before the deadline of December 31, 1969.

Both the architect and the Daly Company submitted their plans
to HUD for approval, and the architect was awarded the Florence project, while the Daly Company got Casa Grande. According to the
architect, HUD's decision was based on his firm's being relatively
small and new in the field; therefore, he was awarded the smaller
project and the Daly Company got the larger one. The 40 units in
Florence were finished in June 1971, by which time ground had not
been broken in Casa Grande.

The Daly Company spent the spring and summer of 1970 unsuccess-
fully looking for money. Some Casa Grande residents were asked to
invest, but they declined because the return on their money was too
low and too slow. Finally, the contract was sold to the Bohemia Lumber Company of Eugene, Oregon. Reportedly, the Daly Company received for architectural services a 5 percent finder's fee (approximately
$200,000, if the report is correct).

During the winter of 1970, startup dates for building the houses
were announced periodically. From January 1971 through June a new
startup date was regularly announced for the 15th of the next month.
On June 17, 1971, PCHA notified Bohemia Lumber Company that its
lease agreement with them was in default as of June 15, 1971. It
was learned that Bohemia had arranged to sell the contract to National
Housing, pending approval of its plans by the PCHA, the City of Casa
Grande's Planning and Zoning Commission, and the City Council.

Also in June 1971, a new developer, Subsidized Housing, entered
the game. PCHA reportedly favored assigning the contract to Subsidized, but on August 8, 1971, National Housing obtained a judgment
in federal court verifying its right to proceed on the housing contract
as Bohemia's legal assignee. National's argument was that it hadn't
had a chance to perform, and it had a legal right to that chance. The
court enjoined the PCHA from interfering with National's efforts to
proceed, and set a date for completion of all 105 houses. According
to PCHA, its "interference" consisted of sending people from Subsidized Housing to Bohemia to see if Bohemia was interested in selling.

Apparently Bohemia showed such a willingness to sell to Subsidized that National brought its lawsuit to prevent that from happening.

National began development of the housing tract in early November 1971, but stopped work after several weeks to negotiate a cost change following the Casa Grande Planning and Zoning Commission's approval of the project contingent on a change in site grading. After this problem was resolved, construction resumed and the first AJC families occupied the residential housing in June 1972. Completion of the housing project continued at a slow pace and final occupation of the residential housing occurred in January 1973, when the 72d AJC family moved in.

The history of the HUD housing project raises a number of interesting questions, the most obvious of which concerns the multiple assignments of the HUD contract. If the first assignment cost was $200,000, the second one must have been at least as much. (One informant mentioned a figure of $350,000.) And if National could not produce the houses under the original contract for the amount HUD was allowing, how could it do so later with $200,000 to $350,000 in additional costs, especially in the wake of greatly increasing building costs over the 18 months between its two ownerships of the contract?

While the firms battled back and forth over who was to make money next, the houses went unbuilt, and AJC was confronted with the serious problem of where to house the AJC families. Ten families were housed in trailers at AJC, and 20 families were put in the Florence project 30 miles away, while the rest were housed in rental units in Casa Grande. Since there were few rental units available there, AJC had to expend a great deal of time and money locating and even refurnishing rental units for the client-families.

The struggle over who had the contract was not the only problem delaying the project. PCHA, as the grant recipient, had the authority to award the building contract but declined to do so, leaving the decision to the HUD regional office, whose lack of knowledge of local conditions further exacerbated the problem. Some elements of the Casa Grande establishment resented the award of the contract to an "outsider" rather than to a local firm. Consequently, rezoning, council approval, issuance of permits, and other matters took longer than might otherwise have been expected.

The lack of anybody clearly in control or responsible for the project also contributed to the delay. At one point, progress was halted pending approval of the pilot plan by the City Council. The plan was on the agenda of four consecutive bimonthly Council meetings before it was brought to the floor. In spite of the importance of City Council action to the project, no representative of AJC, PCHA, or any of the developers involved attended the Council meetings to check on the progress of the pilot plan.

The problems attendant on having to keep the families spread out, and in some cases in substandard housing, have already been well-publicized (see SSS 1971, pp. 10-13).

1. An extra person was needed to help locate and upgrade available rentals (the job developer was the person assigned early in the operational period [February 1971 to February 1972] ; as a result job development was not done during that period).
2. Transportation for families from outlying areas caused many difficulties, especially for those needing medical treatment and for parents with sick children who had to be taken to and from AJC at hours other than those scheduled for regular bus runs; and the costs of the bus service were higher than planned for.
3. The costs of refurbishing private rentals was excessive due to high cleaning deposits and unusually stringent cleanup requirements by the local private landlords .
4. Although the purpose of the AJC housing component is to familiarize the families with the advantages of houses that are not below minimum standards of decency, the available rentals some-times did not meet those standards.
5. Most importantly, the families did not have the opportunity to develop a sense of community by living and working together, an experience designed by the planners of AJC to help in reducing alienation and increase community participation.

Many of the families who lived in the more distant places expressed feelings of dissatisfaction and resentment because they were obliged to spend up to two hours a day or more than the other families due to the extra travel time to and from AJC. They felt them-selves discriminated against by AJC, especially where "unexcused" absences were at issue because messages about illness did not get communicated.

The housing finally became available in February 1973, and almost all the families now live in these new dwelling units. Families are now housed uniformly above minimum standards of decency. The houses are new, and while they leave much to be desired in the quality of their construction, architectural design, room size, and other details, they are in almost all cases superior to the houses families lived in before AJC and the houses in the com-munity which were rented by AJC. Families are allocated houses by family size; the largest house available has four bedrooms. The lives of the larger families, especially, were improved by the move, since there were practically no four-bedroom rentals available in Pinal County.

The dispersion of the families had been a matter of concern from the beginning of regular operations. There was evidence that the first ten pilot families, who lived in the ten residential trailers during their training, had not only enjoyed but made use of their neighborhood environment. Families traded services such as babysitting and minor auto repairs, shopped together, socialized, and generally shared concerns with one another. Many of the people said that the only negative thing about graduation was that they would have to be separated. This was in spite of the fact that all were going to be working at AJC after graduation. Most of the people who felt strongly about the neighborhood ties said that it was the first time they had had this kind of experience. A concomitant of this experience was the fact that AJC had an opportunity to work with the people as a group, rather than only as individuals; the group developed cohesiveness and mutual support systems for dealing with the new information and demands of the job college as they occurred day by day. For example, one young woman in the first ten families spoke of feeling extremely reluctant to leave her preschool children in the Child Development Center (CDC) because she had never been separated from them before. Her distress was not particularly assuaged by being told by the CDC director that the experience would be good for the children. However, learning from some of the other mothers that they shared her feelings helped the young woman to accept the necessity for it and further to involve herself enough to learn how to help her children with new activities at home. The objectives of the CDC in parent education were thus augmented.

Another positive result of the community experience of the first ten families was a change in racial attitudes that came from the direct experience of living and working together. Most people who mentioned these changes made some comment about never having lived with persons of other racial or ethnic backgrounds before and discovering that people are more alike than they expected.

After the relocation of families into the HUD housing was completed, there was a revived interest in the family government organizations. Since the families now lived close enough to each other, getting together for meetings (coupled with the existence of identifiable mutual concerns) became a much more meaningful activity than in the past. Also in recent months, AJC has been encouraging more input from the families relative to job college operations, so the renewed interest in family government has more than one cause; however, much has hinged on the new housing arrangement.

AJC program components are very much enhanced by the housing, since some of the services and training components can now be carried into the home. The Home Living program now has a demonstration house at the housing site, and several of its training segments are carried on in the families' homes.

It is now possible for each counselor to make at least one call each month at the home of every family in his caseload. In addition, visiting families on request is also feasible.

The families can now attend AJC recreational activities at the Esperanza Center (the community center used by AJC) without having to have a car to get there. This is especially helpful when activities for young people are scheduled, because their parents no longer have to transport them back and forth.

Although the housing component was the source of many problems for AJC and for the client families, there are indications in the follow-up data that AJC families are upgrading their housing concomitantly with their incomes. The Home Living program and the housing component of AJC were designed to help change this element of lifestyle, and it appears that they are succeeding even with the less-than-optimum housing AJC was forced to use. We think that the HUD housing should enhance this change. And the help AJC provides in procuring Farmer's Home Administration loans for graduating families, as they already have with some graduates, will further aid these families in acquiring adequate housing.

Recommendations for Replicated Programs. AJC managed to become operational in spite of the delays in the building of the HUD houses, and is to be commended for making the best of a bad situation. However, it has been handicapped by having to take alternative actions, and should be brought under the control of the project, no matter what the funding source is. It was the opinion of the authors over the two and one-half years of construction delays that AJC could and should have exerted pressure on PCHA and the HUD Regional office to cause whoever the contractor was at the time to build the houses, instead of allowing the repeated buying and selling of the contract.

1. The optimum situation would be for a project similar to AJC to assume direct responsibility for the houses. The project could become the developer and subcontract the architectural services and building contracts, and find its own sources of money for developing the project. Its relationship to the local housing authority would then be closer and more one of parity rather than one of total dependence. The project would, of course, have to have a housing department which would be larger and differently staffed than its present structure allows for, but the difficulties might well be outweighed by such advantages as:

- control over actual completion of housing
- the ability to choose to hire local people in the target area
- direct involvement with the local governmental bodies
- involvement in the maintenance of the housing as a result of the project's responsibility for it (the project would become the eventual owner)

• the income that would be available from the HUD subsidy
as well as the project's foreseeably preferential position
in obtaining FHA loans

2. If it did not assume direct responsibility, the project could
still actively involve itself in facilitating the process of getting the
houses built in the local area. If in a new location the housing
authority does not assume its responsibility in matters such as choosing
contractors, and the project is not the developer, the project could
still have staff and others (board members, council members, friends,
and so on) tracking the progress of performance. By becoming informed
about guidelines and other details, the monitors could recognize ir-
regularities and call them to the attention of HUD or attempt to bring
other pressure to bear.

STIPENDS

AJC families are supported by stipends during their training.
The stipend schedule and rent (which is deducted prior to stipend
payment), by family size, is presented below.

Family Size	Monthly Stipend (dollars)	Monthly Rent (dollars)
2	$ 185	$ 50
3	230	60
4	265	60
5	295	65
6	320	65
7	355	70
8	380	70
9	405	75
10	430	75
11	455	75
12	480	75

A budget counselor works with each family to determine how the
stipend is to be spent. Budgeted items listed in Table 3.2 are
deducted from the stipend prior to issuing the family their checks.
Table 3.2 shows how actual stipends were allocated for some AJC
families whose budgets were prepared in October 1973.
Stipend amounts appear to be adequate; the average annual income
reported by graduating-families for their year at AJC was $3511. Based
on the average family size, the average stipend was $3300. Either figure
is considerably higher than the $2694 average annual income reported
by incoming families for the year immediately prior to entering AJC.

TABLE 3.2

Allocation of Stipends

(October 31, 1973)

Family (names deleted)	Stipend	Rent	Food Stamps	Living Expenses[a]	Debt Payment	Net Check[b]
A	132.50	30.00	29.00	17.00	24.00	32.50
B	132.50	30.00	29.00	17.00	15.00	41.50
C	115.00	30.00	13.00	19.00	48.00	5.00
D	115.00	30.00	24.00	14.00	40.00	7.00
E	92.50	25.00	17.00	19.00	—	31.50
F	92.50	25.00	17.00	19.00	—	31.50
G	92.50	25.00	17.00	19.00	—	31.50
H	92.50	25.00	17.00	19.00	—	31.50
I	92.50	25.00	17.00	19.00	15.00	16.50
J	92.50	25.00	17.00	29.00	10.00	14.50
K	160.00	32.50	21.25	46.00	33.00	27.25
L	160.00	32.50	42.50	38.00	42.00	5.00
M	115.00	30.00	24.00	22.00	25.00	14.00
N	115.00	30.00	24.00	22.00	24.00	15.00
O	132.50	30.00	29.00	41.50	10.40	21.60
P	132.50	30.00	29.00	26.50	32.28	14.72

[a]Clothing, car expenses, and miscellaneous expenses (such as recreation).
[b]Stipend less rent, food stamps, living expenses, and debt payment.

Source: Unless otherwise indicated, data for tables have been compiled by the authors.

Historical Notes. Stipends are paid twice each month and since April 1973 have been paid separately to husband and wife as an hourly wage earned by participation in the training program. Before that time, the stipends were paid twice monthly. Families were docked at the rate of 25¢ an hour for unexcused absences from the training programs, and that money was also deducted from the stipends. Since April 1973, a family's stipend is divided by the total number of hours a month that the husband and wife are committed to participate in the program, and that figure becomes the

hourly wage for the adults in the family (the range is from about
$.50 an hour to about $1.30 an hour). Unexcused absences are
now deducted on an hourly basis at the hourly rate at which the
family participates.

Unexcused absences have been a problem at AJC and docking
was initiated early in the program as a method of control. At first,
docking for absences was done quite informally (more as a system
of fines imposed after a pattern of unexcused absences had begun).
Since this procedure tended not to work, appeared rather arbitrary,
and was often only distantly related to the degree of infringement of
the rules, a system was initiated of penalizing unexcused absences
at an established hourly rate.

This new system, in which families earn their stipend by attending
their training activities, has the advantage of being more nearly
modeled on the realities of the noninstitutional world. Parallel
behaviors have similar outcomes (for example, failure to report for
work results in loss of pay just as unexcused failure to report for
training does). The new system also has the advantage of treating
husband and wife as equal partners in the program, with the wife
having equal economic power with her husband. The social/psycho-
logical implications of this kind of parity would make an interesting
study, since, among the Mexican-Americans especially, (though to
a great extent among the other groups too) traditional paternalism is
still quite strong.

Recommendations for Replicated Programs. The actual dollar amount of
the stipends has been the same since AJC began operations. It was
based on the Arizona figures for basic subsistence for welfare payments
in 1970 (Arizona welfare pays two-thirds of the amount considered to
be the minimum; AJC pays the full amount). The cost of living has
been rising at an unprecedented rate (especially over the past 12
months, during which wholesale food prices increased by 39 percent).
Accordingly, it may be necessary to continually reevaluate the stipend
schedule to see if its buying power is adequate for the needs of
families. Otherwise, since one of the criteria for acceptance is
that a family not have so many debts that payments cannot be met by
the stipend, the debt limit (and therefore the number of eligible
families) might have to be reduced. This could be yet another way
of excluding the very poor who are already at the disadvantage in
establishing eligibility for the program. Also, families who are in
the program may be more prone to drop out if the financial pressure
becomes too heavy.

The new system for having families earn the stipend seems to be
sensible and reportedly is having the effect of reducing unexcused
absences. The wide disparity in hourly rates seems to us a potential
problem which may make the equalization of penalty rates advisable.

COUNSELING

The Counseling department consists of six counselors, plus a budget specialist. Organizationally, counseling is part of the Family Services division.

Historical Notes. Counseling at AJC has been a problem area since the very beginning. Until recently, AJC had failed to design a set of policies workable in the context of the client population. For example, since the counselors are assigned the task of assisting families in "decision-making processes," how, other than persuading (telling families what to do) or saying "it is your decision to make," does the counselor go about helping? What are the strategies and learning processes the counselor can use? Until very recently, there have been no formal written answers to the questions, and counseling has been mainly a matter of crisis intervention during or after the crisis. The counselors themselves have had widely ranging educational and experiential backgrounds (from neither experience nor relevant education to Ph.D. candidacy in psychology and/or experience in personal rehabilitation or vocational counseling), and their approaches to counseling have been similarly diverse. Placed in the context of the range of problems AJC families can and do encounter, the highly individualistic counseling procedures provided have been a source of much dissatisfaction among the families and frequently among the counselors themselves.

In addition to these difficulties, caseloads rose as high as 35 families for each counselor (which means approximately 175 people to a counselor, since whole families are included in the counseling load). At the same time, occasional administrative decisions have been handed down to the effect that counselors should concentrate on case coordination (making sure that the families go where they're scheduled to be, and that someone knows whether they do or not), or that counselors should be doing nothing more than "vocational" or "rehabilitation" counseling (neither of those terms had ever been defined, except to stipulate that they exclude "psychological" counseling). In addition, very early in the regular operation phase (starting in February 1971), group counseling was dropped because of its alleged unpopularity with the families. Since the follow-up interviews the ten pilot families produced evidence that many of them found the group counseling the most helpful part of their AJC experience, it seemed rather arbitrary to stop it altogether, as it could have been continued on a voluntary basis.

On going over the client program component evaluations at graduation, individual counseling was rated "most helpful" by 7.2 percent, whereas group and family counseling were each selected as "most helpful" by only 2.7 percent. Family, individual, and group counseling were rated as "not helpful at all" by 9 percent, 4.5 percent, and 18

percent, respectively. The comparatively high negative rating of the
latter is probably due to the fact that most people in the sample had
no group counseling experience at all.

In rating "most helpful" people, counselors were rated relatively
high, which seems to indicate that AJC clients did not perceive that
what the counselors did was counseling, and/or that they experienced
the counselors as helpful individuals without associating them with
their official function. Since the counselors themselves over the years
have expressed high interest in and commitment to the clients, the
dissociation of the counselor as person from counselor as AJC funct-
ionary appears to be reasonable. The counselors' main role often
was that of client advocate when the clients were in trouble with
either the AJC bureaucracy, the outside world, or each other.

The counseling function, early in AJC's history, was set up so
that each family was assigned to a counselor. The initial set of
interviews were to set up program assignments. After that the families
were required to make contact with the counselor at least once a
month. This latter requirement was changed so that no contract with a
counselor was required for a while, and then later it became the
counselor's responsibility to maintain contact. Some families, of
course, had ongoing contact with the counselors, and some had
sporadic contact when there were problems; some families, however,
had practically no counselor contact during the period when none was
required. This loss of contact did not necessarily mean that the
family had no problems; it simply meant that whatever their problems
were, they were not being dealt with, except after some event of
high visibility had occurred.

AJC's efforts to deal with the special problem of alcoholism have
been to require attendance at AA meetings (for alcoholics), to have
drugs and alcohol removed from the AJC premises, and to engage in
individual counseling with individuals known to have such problems.
In cases where symptoms were acute, people are referred to county, state,
and federal facilities. AJC counselors have also participated in
local efforts to educate and provide treatment for young people who
are abusing other drugs.

Early in AJC's history, family planning was treated as a kind of
taboo subject, and insofar as there was any educating done, the
counselors did it in private sessions. This responsibility has since
been taken over by the Medical division as part of its health education
program.

In the past year, the Family Services division has been reorganized. A new emphasis is being placed on the integration of all AJC
services, but especially those within the division, Counseling,
Recruiting, and Job Placement and Development. Three-person teams,
made up of one person from each of the three departments, with the
counselor heading up the team, are now being assigned to each incoming family. The budget specialist works as a consultant to each
team in helping work out family financial obligations within the

limitations of the stipend. The job developers on the teams maintain
periodic contact with "their" families so that job placement will be
the result of a concensus worked out over time, determined by the
acquisition of levels of skills as they relate to the actual job market.

Since the families are now living in the turnkey housing (see the
section "Housing and Maintenance," above), the counselors can
make regular house calls. Previously, with families living all over
the western part of the county, time and distance militated against
the practice. The purpose is to spend some time with the families
when they are all together and thereby gain further insight into their
needs. The counselors report any relevant information to the other
departments. For example, a need for additional furniture would go
to Property Control; or finding that a child is having trouble with a
school subject, the counselor would request tutorial help from Special
Services. In addition to these efforts in care coordination, the counselors hold care conferences with the other divisions once a week
and more frequently in emergencies. The Family Services manager is
also undertaking to coordinate the various departments and divisions
at AJC organizationally, as well as with reference to specific clients,
by means of holding interdepartmental meetings during which staff
people can learn more of the specific capabilities and efforts of one
another, both as individuals and in terms of their functions at AJC.

Recommendations for Replicated Programs. If current and planned
activities continue, the counseling department at AJC will have become fully functional, both for client families and organizationally
for AJC. The two functions are very much interrelated and bear
further examination in the interest of the possibility of replicating
AJC.

AJC has suffered from a lack of coordination of services; and we
have continually strongly recommended that AJC work on organizational
development in the form of improving communications among staff
and between departments. This was especially necessary when the
housing was delayed and the families lived scattered about the county
out of touch with each other and less accessible to AJC than had been
planned for. Keeping track of family needs has been exceptionally
difficult, and the need for open communications among staff has been
even greater than it would have been if all had gone according to plan.
Until recently, AJC has been extremely reluctant to do anything about
internal communications, except to require that things be written
down, thus generating massive amounts of paper.

However, there has been some recent efforts by the Family
Services division to more fully mobilize their own resources for engen-
dering greater internal cooperation. The primary activities in this
respect have been asking staff people themselves to voice their opin-
ions, observations, and feelings, and then soliciting their suggestions
for solving the problems they are encountering. There have been a
number of promising results, including signs of improved morale

and greater energy going into the job itself. There has also been a reduction of paperwork and a greater willingness to experiment with alternate strategies for providing services (such as group counseling).

Organizational development trainers generally use the same skills as group counselors. It is possible that a program such as AJC could develop a model for using internal group counseling resources for continuing organizational development. Such a model might prove to be a practical method for solving some of the organizational problems encountered by programs similar to AJC.

BASIC EDUCATION INSTRUCTION

The term "basic education instruction" as it is used here refers to a variety of different instructional subprograms within the overall AJC program. These include:

1. Adult basic education (ABE): Developmental mathematics, developmental reading, English proficiency training, and courses related to acquiring a GED (a high school equivalency diploma).

2. Vocational-related education: Special courses needed as prerequisities for the vocational training program, such as special mathematics training for carpenters.

3. Life skills: Job readiness, health, hygiene, consumer education, recreation, money management, other similar topics, and home living (sewing, nutrition, home beautification, and so on).

All of these educational components are considered to be important to AJC's "total family rehabilitation" concept, and are described in more detail in the paragraphs immediately below.

Adult Basic Education. All of the activities in this educational component are offered in the Learning Center trailers. These trailers are divided into four separate study areas. The Learning Center started out in one large room, was later divided into two separate locations, with the GED classes in the Esperanza Center and all other activities in a single-room trailer facility, and finally evolved into the present configuration. The need to divide groups was a function of size and the growing numbers of people coming and going with great frequency.

The Learning Center concept was designed to provide individualized study programs for each student, no matter what his or her educational level. Based on the tests given in the Testing and Evaluation Center, students are assigned to whatever area is appropriate for continuing study. At the Learning Center, incoming students are evaluated either by "informal discussion" with the instructor or by means of short proficiency tests which are part of the programmed

instruction materials used in the Learning Center (the Science
Research Associates [SRA] reading and mathematics program). Then
the students begin their courses of study, which are primarily programmed self-teaching materials. Students study as much as three
hours a day in the Learning Center, and many have made substantial
progress; 50 GED's were earned during 1973, 40 in English and ten
in Spanish. Improvements in developmental mathematics and developmental reading have also been made by many students, but these are
difficult to evaluate. There are few benchmarks, and baseline information is available.

Vocational-Related Education. AJC's vocational coordinator is responsible (among other things) for ascertaining prerequisite educational
requirements (if necessary) for all family members enrolled in a
vocational training course. ABE does not necessarily fill this need,
for example, carpentry, drafting, electronics repair, require more
extensive mathematical training than it offers. AJC's policy has been
to purchase vocational-related courses from its training suppliers,
when available. However, AJC has had to provide some of these
courses, even though they are not part of its curriculum, because the
Gila River Career Center (GRCC) has so far not offered sufficient
vocational-related instruction. Since GRCC could provide vocational-
related education more efficiently than AJC, because of its larger
number of participants, AJC has been putting pressure on GRCC to
offer more such courses.

Life Skills. The Life Skills courses encompass a wide variety of
areas. They are taught by personnel from three different divisions,
Instructional, Special Services, and Medical, and are designed to
prepare families for all aspects of middle-class living.
    Life Skills courses offered, by divisions, are listed below.

- Instructional Division: Community Resources, Practice
  Typing, Communication Skills, Measurements, Con-
  sumer Education, Driver's Education, Job Readiness
- Special Services (Home Living): General Family Living
  for Men, General Family Living for Women, Foods I
  and II, Clothing I and II, Care of You and Your Clothes,
  Figure Control, Christmas Sewing, Holiday Cooking,
  Seamstress, Home Beautification
- Special Services (Recreation): Family Recreation I and II,
  Knitting, Ceramics, Painting and Drawing, Volleyball,
  Basketball, Macrame, Rugmaking, Indian Beading,
  Christmas Crafts, Candle Making, Printing, Leather
- Medical: Health I and II, Child Development

The Home Living Component of the Life Skills Program. Because of
AJC's thrust toward "total family rehabilitation," the Home Living
component of the Life Skills program has always received considerable support from AJC management. The notion is that the rehabilitated
(middle-class) family must live in the style that befits its new status,
and that this includes a well-managed, clean, nicely decorated home,
and proper nutrition. AJC's philosophy is that such a home environment, and the resulting pressure from the family to maintain it,
encourages the head-of-household to stay on the job.

The Home Living curriculum has been variously structured over
the three years of AJC's operations but has always been demonstration-
and activity-oriented, rather than purely instructional. And it is the
opinion of the authors that this has been a major strength of the
department, partially because of the average literacy level of the
participant-families, but more because the low-pressure environment
has made Home Living a place where work and pleasure can be
meaningfully associated. In recent months, to meet the requirements
of Central Arizona College, which pays for the instructional hours
of the program, an effort to formalize instructional units has been
initiated. Men have been involved sporadically in Home Living during
the whole history of AJC (mostly in cooking and sewing), but the
present level of involvement is higher than in the past, and introductory subject matter includes home maintenance, cleanliness,
family living, and budget management. This last item is especially
important, now that both husband and wife are direct " wage-earners"
of the family stipend by virtue of participation in AJC (see "stipends, "
above). Home maintenance in the new housing is a major goal of
AJC, both for the preservation of the houses and the upgrading of the
families' lifestyles. Also, AJC management is very sensitive to
community reaction to the appearance of the housing.

Home Living, until the housing became available, maintained
a demonstration home trailer, in addition to a classroom trailer and
cooking and sewing rooms in the Esperanza Center. Since the housing
has become available, there is a demonstration house (the demonstration trailer has since been converted for the Instructional division)
in the housing tract. The house is furnished and decorated as a model
for the families, with the furniture and materials that are available
through AJC or that can be made by the people in their Home Living
or Crafts classes. The demonstration house is used as a classroom
as well as a distribution center for cleaning supplies and small
home furnishings.

The Home Living department also provides homebound teaching
to women who are confined to home for protracted time periods. In
addition, classes are now held occasionally in individual homes,
and some of the women have invited their classes for lunch or other
semisocial occasions.

Staff members of Home Living now make home visitations to help in the achievement and maintenance of order in the families' homes. Equipment and supplies are provided. These staff members also make sure that needed home repairs are reported to maintenance and are taken care of. Part of the purpose of the home visits is to answer questions, to help maintain rapport between staff and families and to reinforce in the home what was learned in the classroom. To that end, Home Living instructors recently attended an inservice training workshop in communication.

Recommendations for Replicated Programs. The Learning Center concept has the advantage of making individualized study possible and is invaluable in as diverse a "school" population as AJC has. However, even the salesmen for programmed materials are quick to point out that these materials do not substitute for human teachers. Unfortunately, AJC has a history of using inexperienced people in the Learning Center, on the assumption that the programmed materials are enough, so there has been too little teacher/student interaction and not much creative curriculum development directly responsive to the student population. As a result, many students have been bored and restless and have tended to spend much time either daydreaming or socializing.

Efforts have been made over the past year to improve the environment of the Learning Center (dividing up groups into separate rooms, dropping the business skills (typing) classes, and initiating Community Resources courses) as well as increasing the number of teachers, and this trend seems to be productive. Teaching strategies and methods of intervention are learned processes, and they are essential skills for teachers (for example, more reading aloud by students has been mentioned as a need). Moreover, the teaching staff needs to be acquainted with other materials available as supplements to the programmed study materials in use in the Center. The incidence of boredom is considerably enhanced by continued repetition of such seemingly unimportant things as the format of printed materials, and an effort should be made to provide some variety. AJC should be building a library of such materials, and students should be guided in their use. Reading as recreation is another area that could be expanded.

The Home Living department has had quite enthusiastic support from the women students at AJC (somewhat less from the men) from the very beginning. Home Living was moderately popular with families in the study sample; 15.3 percent of the individuals interviewed at exit designated the Home Living program as "most helpful," and 65.7 percent reported that it was valuable to their development. There are some positive changes on follow-up that can be attributed to Home Living training. Buying groceries on credit has gone down (from 23 percent to 2 percent) among AJC graduates and not among dropouts; there is increased use of checking accounts (from 10 percent to 23 percent) and savings accounts (from 17 percent to 44 percent). The purchase of life insurance has gone up slightly (from 8 percent to 12 percent) among graduates but not among dropouts.

The data also show a great increase in sewing during the training period (53 percent of the families reported they sewed more), and there is some carryover in this activity after graduation (eight months after graduation, 20 percent were still sewing). One reason for this drop is that AJC students were taught sewing on very complicated, expensive sewing machines, which they cannot afford to duplicate for private use. AJC recently, however, has purchased two new inexpensive machines; participants in the home living program selected the machines in a comparative shopping experiment.

VOCATIONAL TRAINING

Vocational training at AJC is purchased almost completely from 13 outside training schools. One of the important questions of this study is whether locating AJC centrally for the client population without full internal vocational training facilities is a feasible plan. The answer is a qualified "yes"—if there are enough vocational training resources accessible to the project within a reasonable distance.

The primary advantage of purchasing, rather than providing training internally, is that a much wider variety of vocational choices can be given without the expense of trying to develop even a minimal set of courses. This latter aspect is very important. AJC seems to have reached an optimum operating level with something between 70 and 80 families, not a big enough "school" population to allow for an extensive curriculum, but too many to confine to only a half-dozen vocational training courses.

A list of the 36 available vocational training courses is contained in Appendix B.

Historical Notes. In the early operational phases of AJC (February to September 1971), vocational training plans for client-families were slow in developing, partly because little had been done ahead of time to explore and evaluate training schools, arrangements with Central Arizona College (CAC, the local community college) had not been agreed upon, and the Gila River Career Center (administered by CAC) was not yet functioning.

Some families, during the early stage of AJC's operations, were in the program for more than four months before they were assigned to a vocational training program. AJC counselors attributed the high dropout rate to excessive delays in starting the families' vocational training. Some of the training programs turned out to be inadequate, and changes had to be made. AJC began giving some of the training courses in-house (such as beginning carpentry, auto mechanics, and plumbing), but these efforts were not entirely satisfactory. Classes were not divided by level of competence and the teachers were inexperienced. These courses have since been moved to the Gila River Career Center (GRCC).

The situation began to change in the spring of 1972, when the GRCC began to become operational (full-scale operations began in fall/winter, 1972). GRCC is a vocational training facility located on the Gila River Indian Reservation, 15 miles from AJC. It was originally planned as an Indian job training facility, but it has turned out that the number of Indian students is not large enough to sustain the school, so the student population has become about 50 percent non-Indian.

When GRCC had just started operations, the number of AJC trainees was a large proportion (50 percent) of the total student population. AJC therefore was able to have a very substantial influence on the selection of instructors and courses, and on course content. By June 1973 the total GRCC student population was 260, 60 of whom were AJC students. Although the fraction of GRCC students who are AJC has diminished, GRCC remains sensitive to AJC's special needs.

The cost of training at GRCC is $1.50 for each student training hour, and the vocational training is paid for by the state Division of Vocational Rehabilitation.

The efficacy of GRCC training has improved since its founding, due to its becoming stabilized with more secure funding, thus giving it the opportunity to develop its own resources. In addition, AJC now has people from its Counseling and Job Development staffs monitoring the AJC students at GRCC (on-site) to assist them in whatever ways are possible to cope more effectively with the training programs.

In addition to the purchased training from the outside training sources in Pinal and Maricopa Counties, AJC utilizes TOJ (training on the job without pay) and OJT (on-job training with pay) with local employers. AJC still does some training on-site, in those areas where trainees can participate in AJC's operations; this involves maintenance work and positions such as dental aide, cook's helper, maintenance, home help aide, and child care aide.

Job training at AJC, in spite of all the problems in the past, has been successful. In 1973, 58 graduates were placed in non agricultural jobs. Of these, 51 (or 88 percent) were in training-related jobs. Data on the 105 sample families revealed that, of 46 graduates who had been placed prior to the exit interview, 29 (or 63 percent) had been placed in training-related jobs. Furthermore, 41 (or 68 percent) out of a subsample of 60 individuals from the study sample were placed in either the vocational training program of their choice or an alternate program recommended by the psychometrist. Thus, most trainees were able to get the kind of training they wanted and most were placed in training-related jobs.

When the AJC trainees were asked to evaluate various program components, they rated vocational training by far the most helpful; 31.5 percent designated it as such.

Recommendations for Replicated Programs . The location of AJC outside a metropolitan area appears to be workable in its particular case, where a junior college and a skills training center are close at hand, and other vocational training resources are within commuting distance 45 miles away in Tempe and Phoenix.

Replicated programs would do well to develop their vocational training sources and programs before accepting their first client-families. Delays in beginning vocational training was a major reason for many families becoming discouraged and dropping out of AJC.

THE CHILD DEVELOPMENT CENTER

AJC's Child Development Center (CDC) is a licensed daycare facility with two objectives. The first is to provide child care for AJC families so that both husband and wife can participate full time in the AJC program, and the second is to contribute to the physical, emotional, and mental development of AJC children.

Children are segregated into seven different age groups. The age ranges, the number of children allowed in each group's daily attendance, and the number of staff persons working with each group are as follows:

Age Group	Number Licensed For	Staff Size
6 weeks-18 months	30	5
18 months-2 years	12	2
2 years-2.5 years	12	2
2.5 years-3.25 years	12	2
3.25 years-4 years	12	1
4 years-Kindergarten	15	2
Kindergarten	22	1

The department is headed by a very well-qualified child development specialist, and several experienced teachers serve on the staff. In addition, the CDC benefits from the services of several volunteers.

Administratively, the Child Development Center is part of the Medical division.

AJC's CDC is similar to a Head Start program (although AJC has never been able to procure any funding from Head Start). A variety of materials and toys are available to enhance the children's mental and cultural development. Nutritious lunches and snacks are provided during the day. the CDC has a well-equipped playground for outdoor activities.

Child development is, of course, an important part of "total family rehabilitation." AJC hopes that the preschool children of its families will gain enough through their CDC experience to later, in public school, equal the achievements of other middle-class children (they presumably will be middle class when they enter public school). With the current CDC supervisor, AJC has the best chance in its history to achieve the second objective of its child development program (above), to contribute to the physical, emotional, and mental development of the children of its client-families.

Historical Notes. AJC's daycare center was originally housed (before completion of the neighborhood facility) in a very small area of the trailer complex. The worst problem in those days was overcrowding. Completion of the neighborhood facility alleviated that problem, but as the number of children increased another problem arose, diarrhea. Parents complained that their children contracted diarrhea (and lice) in the daycare center and did not want to leave them there. This, in turn, caused some parents to miss part of the program while they tended to their sick children.

There has always been a certain amount of resistance among AJC families to leaving their children in the daycare center. The younger mothers have been especially reluctant to leave their babies there for the first time. Thus, it is difficult to say whether the health problems in the center the parents have always complained about are as bad as they sound, or simply that parents, because of negative feelings toward the idea of daycare, overreact to any sign of illness in their children that could be attributable to the daycare center. Whatever the reason, the problems of ill health in AJC children prompted an administrative change, in which the CDC was transferred from the Family Services division to the Medical division.

The Medical division manager contends that all of the health problems associated with the CDC have been solved. He attributes the persistant diarrhea complaint to the poor dietary habits of the families who have just entered the program and have not yet been through the nutrition classes.

Parents in the study sample gave the CDC a generally high rating. Fourty-six percent of those responding said it was the most valuable part of the program for their children and 10 percent said it was the "most helpful" component for their family as a whole. Over 50 percent rated the CDC personnel as well-qualified.

Recommendations for Replicated Programs. Client-families of programs similiar to AJC have to be sold by the program on the idea of daycare.

The most spectacular economic gains among AJC graduate-families
have been made by families where both parents are employed after
graduation. Also, vocational training for the wives is good insurance
for society against possible expenditures of Aid to Dependent Children (ADC) funds in the future. In order for the wives to get this
training and apply it later, they must be convinced that their children
will benefit from daycare.

AJC has been fairly successful in its daycare operations. One
of the better aspects is the child care aide training program, which
gets the parents involved in the daycare operation. This involvement
gives the CDC good publicity among the families and, at the same
time, provides some training for the parents.

As was mentioned above in "Orientation," the CDC's part of
orientation should be the first item on the program, in order to help
alleviate any uneasiness parents have about leaving their children
in the daycare center.

CHILD SERVICES

The functions of the Child Services program component are to
structure school-age children's after-school time, provide tutoring
for school-age children who require it, perform liaison activities with
school officials, teachers, and others in similar positions, and
provide special programs for children with severe behavioral problems.

AJC has a very active after-school program for school-age
children, including Boy and Girl Scout programs, cultural enrichment,
crafts, 4-H, free play, and field trips. These activities fill the
need of daycare services for school-age children during non-school hours
and, at the same time, provide the normal after-school activities that
middle-class children participate in. VISTA workers staff the after-
school program.

The tutoring of AJC children is done in their classrooms during
school hours and under their teacher's supervision. Six adults from
the AJC families, three men and three women, go to the school every
day. These tutoring services provided by AJC are open to all school-
children, whether they are children of AJC families or not. Thus,
this program is an important part of AJC's community participation.
The individuals who go to the schools are scheduled by the VISTA
worker who coordinates the program.

A VISTA worker also goes to the schools each day to respond to
any emergencies involving AJC children, such as disciplinary problems
or illness occurring during the day. School officials thus have someone to call to respond to unusual events involving AJC children. The
VISTA worker serves as a surrogate parent in this respect.

The Child Services program also operates special programs for
AJC children of all ages who are very antagonistic or very withdrawn,
and hence unable to participate in the regular activities of the daycare

programs at AJC. A psychologist from Arizona State University has been retained as a consultant to this program.

AJC's Child Services program is administratively part of the Special Services division.

Historical Notes. AJC has always provided after-school activities for its school-age children. This has, in the past, included a "teen room" with a pool table and a record player (although the current group of AJC families are so young that there are currently only a very few teen-age children). AJC has experimented with after-school tutoring and extra reading classes, but found that an extended school day was too confining and exhausting for most children. Hence the present format evolved, with the tutoring taking place during school hours and the after-school time being devoted to recreational activities.

The liaison activities were more demanding in the past, before the turnkey housing became available. AJC children who lived in Casa Grande were scattered among three different elementary schools (now all attend the same elementary school). Children of families who lived in Florence were bussed to Casa Grande every day with their parents, and attended Casa Grande schools. Sometimes the busses were late, making the children tardy, and requiring official excuses. These children were also more easily tired out because of the early-morning bus ride and tended to be more of a problem in school.

AJC family members rated the Child Services recreational program high. Twenty-two and five-tenths percent listed it as "most helpful" for their children. The tutorial program was listed as "most helpful" by only nine percent (it is to be hoped that this was because only a few children required tutoring).

Recommendations for Replicated Programs. AJC's Child Services program, as it now operates, appears to be working well. The after-school tutoring component, in AJC's original plans, was abandoned for a more extensive after-school recreational program.

When AJC began operating, school officials in Casa Grande were a bit uneasy about the sudden concentration of children from disadvantaged families being placed in their schools. The liaison efforts of the VISTA workers assigned to AJC's Child Services program has been invaluable in contributing to the schools' and the community's acceptance of AJC school-age children. Programs using AJC as a model would do well to emulate AJC's current Child Services program in its entirety.

JOB DEVELOPMENT AND PLACEMENT

The Job Development and Placement department (JDP) has the responsibility for finding employment for AJC graduates and for providing follow-up placement services for up to three years after graduation. The department consists of three workers. JDP also is responsible for locating TOJ (training on job; one week, unpaid) and OJT (on-job training; up to one month, paid) for AJC students during the latter phase of their participation in the AJC program. These placements are made with the hope they will lead to permanent employment. In recent months, JDP has become increasingly more involved in working with families in job-seeking and retention skills, beginning during the early phase of training and planning for continuous skills development during each student's time at AJC.

AJC had also planned for JDP to do an area survey of current and projected job opportunities so that training for AJC families would be related to the needs of local industry. However, a similar survey was recently made by the Casa Grande Union High School. AJC is now using the results of this survey.

The job developers' tasks include searching out actual job openings in the areas preferred by job-seeking clients (primarily the Casa Grande area, but extending to Phoenix and Tucson). This entails using the resources of the state employment offices in the appropriate geographical areas, as well as contacting employers directly for information on current and prospective employment openings in their businesses. Total number of employer contacts were averaging about 100 per month by the end of 1972. Placements, including TOJ and OJT, averaged 10 a month at that time.

The job developers have also begun to enter into the matter of starting wage levels and have recently told some employers they could not place AJC people with them because they were offering too little. In one case, this had the effect of raising the starting rate from $1.65 an hour to $2.50 an hour. The job developers' responsibilities also include working directly with AJC trainees, helping them to fill out applications, and getting them to and from interviews.

AJC's approach to job development includes teaching such things as grooming, reading and filling out applications, and interviewing techniques (using videotape feedback). First-hand explorations of "the world of work" are made by means of field trips and presentations by local employers. All of the foregoing are covered in daily sessions during the family's first month at AJC. Both husband and wife are exposed to this part of the program even if the wife does not wish to obtain vocational training and a job upon graduation.

JDP also coordinates with the Instructional division and their vocationally-related curriculum so that specific individual client needs can be met as they occur.

Continuing contact is made with family members during their

training year, with emphasis on how and where to look for jobs (state employment offices, newspapers, and direct applications to employers). Private employment agencies' fee practices are explained (use of these agencies is generally discouraged).

One of the job developers is assigned to spend part of each week at the main job training site, the Gila River Career Center. The main purpose of these on-site visits is to coordinate client counseling at the Career Center. The visits also give JDP staff greater opportunity to provide input to the actual vocational training AJC family members are getting. For example, due to some disappointing experiences in placing previous graduates, the job developers have become critical of the non-production-related way certain industrial skills are being taught; this information has been relayed to the vocational teachers.

Historical Notes. JDP was one of the last functions to be started at AJC, primarily because the efforts of the department were sidetracked into helping with housing, which was a special problem until early 1973 (see "Housing and Maintenance" above). Sporadic efforts were made during the first year of AJC's regular operations (February 1971 to February 1972) to teach students job-getting skills and interviewing techniques (mostly in the Instructional program), but, by and large, early graduates of AJC had very little training in that area. Also, without an area industrial survey, job training selections were not made on the basis of area needs, so that training-related placements were often difficult to find. This was especially true of people who had been trained in "marginal marketable skills" (such as parent/ child center aide, or home living aide).

The job developers started becoming more involved in the total delivery of family services (described more fully in "Counseling" above) in mid-1972. As a result, incoming families came in direct contact with the whole idea of job development from the very beginning of their attendance at AJC (as opposed to the first group of families who graduated in February 1972, some of whom didn't even know that job development and placement were part of AJC's program).

The authors analyzed the reported activities of JDP by events for the four-month time period between May and August of 1972. The following frequency distribution provides some insight into how JDP allocated its efforts over its various activities:

Activity	Frequency	(percent)
Initial contacts with potential employers	27	(9.7)
Follow-up contacts with potential employers	80	(29.3)
Arranging interviews	8	(2.9)
Arranging OJT and TOJ	12	(4.4)
Contacts with employers on specific jobs for AJC graduates	19	(7.0)

Activity	Frequency	(percent)
Contacts with other agencies (such as DVR, DES, and GRCC)	56	(20.5)
Follow-up contacts with employers with AJC graduates on the payroll	16	(5.9)
Internal (to AJC) contacts with staff in regard to families' training plans	24	(8.8)
Contacts with AJC families in training: preparation for interviews, resume preparation, and other similiar activities	31	(11.4)
Total	273	(100.0)

Recent discussions with JDP staff indicate that the activities listed above still occupy most of their time with their efforts distributed according to roughly the same percentages.

In the study sample, 58 graduate-husbands responded to the question, "Did AJC assist you in getting a job?" Of these, 42 (72 percent) responded "yes." As JDP functions become more visible, this fraction will undoubtedly increase.

Tables 3.3 and 3.4 present data on the placement of AJC graduates in training-related jobs. Table 3.3 contains data from interviews with families in the study sample, most of whom (all but 3) were graduating in 1972 or dropping out in 1971 and 1972. The percentage of training-related jobs for male (indicated by columns marked "M") graduates is in the 55 to 70 percent range at all three measurements. For female graduates, generally about half of the job placement are training-related. Data from AJC follow-up records were used to develop Table 3.4, which shows that training-related job placements were achieved in 89 percent of all cases in its time period for men and between 70 percent and 80 percent for women. Apparently JDP is improving its operations.

A comparison of AJC graduates with AJC dropouts in Table 3.3 shows some striking differences. The percentage of training-related job placements for dropouts is mostly zero, with the only nonzero measurement being for men at the time of exit (28 percent).

For Table 3.3, the low ratio of row 2 responses to the number of interviews in row 1 for men on graduation is accounted for by the fact that the exit interviews conducted by the research team often took place in the last week before graduation, and job placements had not yet been arranged. In fact, of the first graduating class (February 1972), more than 50 percent were not placed three days before graduation, though in part as a result of the authors' discovering this fact, the job developer secured employment (not necessarily training-related) for most of that group within the following week.

TABLE 3.3

Placements in Training-Related Jobs—1972 AJC Graduates and Dropouts

	Exit		4 Month		8 Month		Exit		4 Month		8 Month	
	M	F	M	F	M	F	M	F	M	F	M	F
Number of families interviewed	62	14	41	20	22	10	16	3	7	1	5	1
Number employed	32	14	36	20	22	10	14	3	9	1	3	1
Percent of employed who are in training-related jobs	66	57	67	45	73	50	29	0	0	0	0	0

TABLE 3.4

Placements in Training-Related Jobs—1973 AJC Graduates

	Exit		Follow-up*	
	M	F	M	F
Number working	47	11	35	7
Percent working in training-related jobs	89	82	89	71

* Average time between graduation and follow-up: 6.5 months

Recommendations for Replicated Programs. AJC appears to be improving its job placement and development functions considerably, and if
current activities are maintained and current plans implemented, it
seems likely that at least some of the families who have shown little
or no improvement in their socioeconomic status may increase their
success rates in the future. In addition, with improved contacts with
business and industry, it seems likely that AJC could expect increasing opportunities for better jobs in those enterprises where AJC graduates have been successful. Also, the increasing coordination between
JDP and the vocational training activities is good for current trainees,
in that training-related difficulties in making placements can be fed back
directly to the trainers who, hopefully, can modify their programs
accordingly, thus making their students more employable.

If AJC were to be replicated, job development and placement
should begin earlier, with both client services and an area employment survey, as well as the establishment of contacts with prospective employers. The proposed Industrial Advisory Council, originally
conceived as a sort of an advisory board made up of local potential
employers, never quite became functional. The biggest problem was
that the Council had no clear-cut objectives regarding what it could
do to help implement the AJC JDP activities, other than maintain good-
will toward the project.

Another need of the job developers has been printed materials for
employers. The recently developed brochure will be useful for giving
a general picture of what AJC is all about. However, some way of
presenting hard data being collected by the follow-up coordinators
(see the next section, "Follow-up") should be planned for on a continuing basis as a supplement. Both presently participating and prospective employers need to have the sense of reward which is rein-
forced by such information.

The fact that Casa Grande has recently become something of a
boom town with new businesses and industries willing and able to
take on trained AJC graduates has made JDP's job easier. The importance of the local employment picture for the success of AJC graduates
is not only that employment is available but that by making it possible
for people to avoid having to move away for jobs, the familiar social
supports of family and community can be sustained, and follow-up
services can be made available (such as AJC's health program).
Unfortunately, not every replicated program will find itself in such
a pleasant economic environment.

                                FOLLOW-UP

Two follow-up coordinators perform an ongoing survey of AJC
graduates and terminees. They collect data on wages and wage

increases, keep track of the health status of families, note job changes and promotions, and maintain up-to-date addresses for families. When required, the follow-up coordinators perform some counseling and assist families in problem-solving. The latter function often involves referring a family to a social service agency for help. In particular, if adult family members are unemployed, the follow-up coordinators work with JDP to place the individual in another job.

The follow-up coordinators also serve as internal program evaluators. Some limited processing of data is performed for display on a large chart on the wall of the follow-up coordinators' office. Table 3.5 presents a sample of some of the salary data that are processed and displayed. Data of this type are also used in such things as applications and public relations releases.

Historical Notes. The follow-up activity at AJC, although originally in the program design, was not actually implemented until 1973. Before that time, counselors occasionally would call a graduate-family on the telephone, or a graduate would drop by AJC to see a friend, but no formal follow-up function was performed.

The lack of a formal follow-up activity is evident in the follow-up data gathered for the evaluation research project. On the four-month follow-up survey of the study sample, of the 32 graduate-husbands who responded to the question "Are you working now?" five answered "no," an unemployment rate of 16 percent. After eight months, this unemployment rate had increased to 33 percent out of a sample of 24 graduate-husbands who responded. The study sample was made up of 105 families who were admitted early in AJC's operational phase, between February 1971 and April 1972. Hence the husbands in the samples cited above graduated between February 1972 and April 1973. For 1973, the first year that the follow-up program was operational, statistics published by the follow-up coordinators and JDP at the end of the year indicate that five out of the 47 graduate-husbands surveyed by the follow-up coordinators were unemployed (11 percent). This lower unemployment rate provides evidence that supports the assertion that the follow-up activity is valuable.

Recommendations for Replicated Programs. Programs can delay setting up a follow-up activity until they have some graduates or terminees to follow up on. AJC, however, waited too long (the follow-up efforts of the evaluation research field interviews provided a reason for AJC to not do follow-up work; however, these field interviews were no substitute for a good follow-up program). Follow-up activity should be organized prior to the first graduation. There will undoubtedly be some terminees who can benefit from follow-up services before the first graduate has left the program. One follow-up coordinator will suffice at the beginning. However, as the graduate and terminee population increases, additional follow-up coordinators will be required.

TABLE 3.5

Statistics on AJC Graduate-Families
Developed by Follow-up Coordinators

| Month | Number of Graduates | | | Average Hourly Wages (dollars) | | | | |
| | | | | Training-Related Jobs | | Non-training-Related Jobs | | Pre-AJC |
	Men	Women	Children	Men	Women	Men	Women	
1972								
February	12	13	47	3.14	1.70	2.16	–	1.49
April	6	7	16	3.50	–		–	1.89
June	21	24	86	3.60	2.12	3.16	1.25	1.84
August	7	7	22	3.91	2.18	2.31	–	1.83
October	10	10	33	3.13	–	2.27	1.60	1.50
December	4	6	18	2.91	2.07	1.50	–	1.55
1973								
January	12	13	42	3.63	1.90	3.14	1.43	1.90
March	13	13	63	2.67	2.00	2.25	–	1.50
April	5	5	11	3.25	–	2.75	2.10	1.32
May	4	4	11	3.30	–	–	–	1.87
June	3	3	6	2.68	–	–	–	1.77
July	9	9	35	2.60	–	–	–	1.48
August	5	5	10	3.17	–	–	1.65	1.45
September	3	3	17	2.50	–	2.00	–	1.75
October	5	5	12	2.71	2.16	2.00	–	1.41
November	1	1	2	2.75	–	–	–	2.00

In order to estimate the maximum number of follow-up coordinators that will eventually be required, it is necessary to first estimate the following quantities:

V: average number of follow-up visits before a family is totally self-sufficient required for each family in the population to be served

T: average time between visits to an individual family

F: average number of follow-up visits a follow-up counselor can make during each time unit (a "time unit" being that which T is expressed in, weeks, months, and so on)

E: average rate at which families exit from the program, in families for each time unit.

Then, assuming the first visit is made T months after exit, the number of follow-up counselors ultimately required can be estimated using the following formula:

$$C = [V(T+1)] \, (E/F).$$

For example, if a program estimates that three follow-up contacts, on the average, will be required before a family is self-sufficient; follow-up contracts should be made every other month; a follow-up coordinator can make two visits each day, or about 40 visits each month; and families, both graduates and terminees, exit from the program at an average rate of ten each month, then $V=3$, $T=2$ months, $F=40$ visits each month, and $E=10$ families each month. Using the formula printed above,

$$C = [3(2+1)](10/40) = 1.75.$$

Hence, two follow-up coordinators would be required, in this hypothetical situation, in order to sustain the level of follow-up service specified above.

MEDICAL PROGRAM

AJC's Medical program serves an approximately equal number of AJC families and non-AJC migrant and seasonal farm worker families. AJC staff members and their families can also receive medical care at the facility as a fringe benefit for a nominal fee ($5 annually for the staff member plus $2 annually for each family member). The facility, which is very well equipped, includes medical and dental receiving rooms, a pharmacy, hospital beds, and offices. A full-time physician, a fulltime dentist (provided by the National Health Service Corps), a fulltime pharmacist, and several nurses are all available to the beneficiaries of this program. The division is well managed and an excellent supporting staff is maintained.

In addition to the facilities at AJC, the AJC Health Services division runs an extensive outreach operation. This outreach program includes several components:

1. Family health assistance. Three to six staff members visit about 280 target population families each month to provide counseling in general family health care; this program includes follow-up visits to AJC graduate families.

2. Family planning. In Maricopa County, AJC provides services in the homes of migrant families in the areas of pre- and postnatal care for mothers and newborn infants, as well as information on birth control methods.

3. Immunization. A registered nurse travels around the area accompanied by an interpreter in a telephone-equipped van administering diptheria-tetanus boosters and other injections to fieldworkers in the agricultural fields and migrant workers' families in the labor camps.

AJC's Medical program recently was selected as the first program to be allowed to include hospitalization services (up to 90 days per year) under its grant from the Migrant Health Service. There will eventually be seven such demonstration programs. AJC has arranged with the local Hoemako Hospital to provide the hospitalization services, for which Hoemako will be reimbursed by AJC from AJC's medical grant funds. The provision exists for AJC to refer clients to larger hospitals in the Phoenix area if the need arises.

Eligibility for AJC's Medical program is determined, within the guidelines specified in the grant, by the Fee, Rate, and Admissions Committee. This committee is composed of one member from AJC's Board of Directors, one consumer, and one Health Services division staff member. Priorities for acceptance for care and treatment are the following:

1. AJC families
2. DVR clients enrolled in the AJC "day-student" program (see p. 208-09)
3. in-migrants (migrant families moving into the area)
4. elderly poor on fixed incomes
5. emergencies
6. others, as space and time permit

Beneficiaries are billed for services provided by AJC's clinic according to "base units." Base units are measures of effort for each type of encounter; the California Code (for standard charges of insurance reimbursement for medical services) is used to determine the number of base units attributable to each visit to the AJC Clinic. Bills for services are calculated on the basis of $8 a base unit. After each bill is prepared, if the billee is eligible for benefits under AJC's grant, then his bill is credited by the proper amount. The credited amount is determined by an "ability to pay" scale which is a function of family income and family size. For example, a family of five whose income is $450 per month pays 30 percent of its bills up to $140.00, beyond which it pays nothing.

AJC has demonstrated that its Medical Services division is self-supporting in that if the total amounts billed to clients were actually collected, the cost of operating the division's medical facilities would be covered.

Appendix C presents a breakdown of encounters (activities) of AJC's Health Services division for fiscal year 1973.

The AJC staff medical program is also operated by the Health Services division.

Free medical care is provided to all AJC graduates for 90 days after graduation. Therefore AJC graduate-families are visited by family health assistants 6, 9, 12, 24, and 36 months after graduation.

Dropouts also receive follow-up care. Ironically, since dropouts often continue to qualify as migrant or seasonal farmworkers, they sometimes receive medical care for a longer period of time than AJC graduates.

A good example of how well AJC has been accepted in the community has been the recent request, by the city of Casa Grande, that AJC's Health Services division set up a Local Alcoholic Rehabilitation Center (LARC) to serve the city of Casa Grande. As of January 1, 1974, when alcoholism was no longer considered a crime, jails were ruled out as detoxification facilities, and hence every community was called upon to set up a LARC. The city turned to AJC for help and AJC responded quickly to this urgent need, deferring the question of how the city would reimburse AJC for the costs involved, which were considerable. A trailer was converted into a suitable detoxification center and by January 9, 1974, Casa Grande's LARC unit had already had 11 "clients." The LARC unit is manned around the clock by AJC staff. City police now bring drunks to the LARC instead of booking them in the city jail.

Historical Notes. AJC's medical program began operating in fiscal year 1971, with a grant from the Arizona Public Health Service. Before that time, AJC utilized the Casa Grande Clinic as its health services resource. Since the OEO grant did not allow payments for medical services, AJC utilized its Ford Foundation money, and in some cases its DVR money, for its families' medical expenses.

An early attempt by AJC to fully utilize the Pinal County Public Health Services (PCPHS) created some bad feelings. AJC was accused of overtaxing the PCPHS Casa Grande Office, while AJC regarded its use of this facility as mobilization of a community resource. As a result, the Casa Grande Office of the PCPHS was closed for a period of time. These unfortunate events occurred at a time when AJC was striving for community acceptance. The altercation between AJC and PCPHS was evidently settled amiably, however, for the former head of PCPHS later became AJC's first staff physician.

Recommendations for Replicated Programs. AJC's medical program is excellent. It has been able to obtain adequate financial support by becoming one of the health centers funded by the Migrant Health Service. Similar programs would do well to emulate AJC's methods (such as superior grantsmanship and convenient location) in achieving equal success.

Early in AJC's history it became evident that, if the families were to have adequate medical care at a cost that the program could afford, AJC would have to set up its own clinic. The authors feel that this will be true of any similar program. Thus, if it is infeasible for the program to have its own medical component, the program managers might consider locating near one of the Migrant Health Services' facilities, or a similar facility for which the program's clients could be eligible (such as the neighborhood health centers that used to be funded by OEO before its transferral to HEW).

VISTA AT AJC

The most valuable resource mobilized by AJC has been the VISTA workers. Since their introduction into regular AJC staff positions early in the program's history, they have provided a variety of sorely needed professional services to AJC, and a considerable amount of talent, education, and dedication. They have a unique position in that they are not seeking career development through working at AJC (although many stay on as regular staff members after their VISTA assignments have expired); their main objective is being at AJC is to serve in ameliorating poverty. Because of this special role, they can contribute to AJC in ways that the program desperately needs. For example, they can pinpoint areas that need improvement and suggest ways to effect changes without endangering their own careers. Thus, they have on occasions served AJC an an effective internal evaluation unit.

At the time of writing there were 19 VISTA volunteers in service at AJC. They filled a variety of positions in several divisions. Table 3.6 has been prepared to illustate the number and nature of important functions performed by VISTAs at AJC.

AJC also has a fulltime VISTA supervisor. His duties include:

- all administrative tasks, paperwork, and other similar tasks required by ACTION (agency containing Peace Corps, VISTA, and so on)
- scheduling such things as vacations, and sick leave for AJC's VISTAs
- distributing information to volunteers, implementing policies, and similar work
- liaison work between the volunteers, ACTION, and AJC
- counseling volunteers
- serving in an advocacy role to AJC on behalf of the volunteers' work

The last duty listed above is important because it assures that AJC will maximize the volunteers' skills, rather than place them in menial tasks.

VISTAs, being volunteers, often "volunteer" (by default) to perform most of the off-hours extra-duty functions required of AJC staff members. In particular VISTAs currently teach an evening sewing class, coordinate evening teen-age recreation programs, act as advisors to (evening) family government meetings, provide evening home visits in home living instruction, monitor City Council meetings (in the evening), and

TABLE 3.6

Vista Positions and Duties at AJC

Division	Positions	Duties
Administration	1. community relations coordinator	publicity, media relations, brochure preparation, grantmanship
Housing and Maintenance	2. assistant housing specialist	all duties of Housing Manager
Instructional Services	3. Learning Center teacher	developmental math assistance
	4. Learning Center teacher	developmental reading assistance
	5. teacher – Life Skills	consumer education
	6. Learning Center teacher	English as second language, citizenship
	7. Learning Center teacher	GED courses
Family Services	8. follow-up coordinator	see coordinates follow-up work with graduates and terminees
	9. follow-up coordinator	coordinates follow-up work with graduates and terminees
	10. counselor	counsels AJC residential families
	11. counselor	counsels AJC residential families
	12. counselor	counsels AJC day students and assists in administering the day student program
	13. special teacher	works with children who have special behavioral problems
Special Services	14. teacher – Life Skills	teaches home living
	15. child services volunteer	coordinates tutoring program
	16. child services volunteer	liaison with school officials
	17. recreation volunteer]	[teaches arts and crafts courses and
	18. recreation volunteer]	[organizes special events for families
Health Services	19. LPN	regular nursing, teaching, Family Planning counseling, trains Health Aides, other similar duties.

provide formal counseling in the evening. VISTAs also serve as 4-H club leaders, Boy and Girl Scout leaders, and Brownie and Cub Scout leaders. All in all, the presence of the VISTAs at AJC enriches the experience for both the families and regular staff members as well as providing a significant economic benefit to the program.

Historical Notes. AJC received its first group of 12 VISTAs in fiscal 1971. There were some early problems caused by AJC's not being willing to use the VISTAs as full professionals. (There was some complaining among the VISTAs that AJC was using them soley to change dirty diapers in the daycare center.) The volunteers' considerable skills, however, soon became noticed and AJC before long was using the VISTAs to their full capacities.

Late in fiscal year 1973, the VISTAs published a critique of AJC, which pointing out a number of what they perceived as deficiences. Largely as a result of this document, the number of VISTAs at AJC was increased from 12 to 22.

Recommendations for Replicated Programs. Programs similar to AJC would do well to coordinate with ACTION very early in their planning phase in order to ascertain how to apply for VISTA help and to determine the level of assistance that VISTA can provide. Mobilization of such a valuable resource early in a program's history is important for the planning phase, particulary from a budgetary sense. At AJC, for example, the impact on AJC's budget would be catastrophic if the VISTAs suddenly became unavailable and had to be replaced by paid professional staff members. A program that is just getting started might be able to begin operations much sooner if it is able to obtain the level of assistance from VISTA that AJC has.

CLIENT EVALUATIONS OF PROGRAM COMPONENTS

Individuals in the families in the study sample were asked in the exit interview "How would you rate the (name of program component, such as Learning Center) in helping you to achieve your goals?" Possible responses, by numerical code, were:

1: extremely valuable
2: quite valuable
3: slightly valuable
4: neither
5: slightly worthless
6: quite worthless
7: extremely worthless.

TABLE 3.7

Program Component Evaluation

Program Component	Usefulness		Personnel		Rate	
	Graduates	Dropouts	Graduates	Dropouts	Graduates	Dropouts
Vocational Training	2.20	3.11*	2.28	3.19*	3.89	4.00
Learning Center	3.03	3.58	2.67	3.75*	4.05	4.58
Child Development Center	2.52	3.12	2.60	3.39*	3.90	4.44*
Home Management Training	2.57	3.4*	2.51	3.38*	3.79	4.29
Individual counseling	2.98	3.97*	-	-	-	-
Family counseling	3.28	3.73*	-	-	-	-
Group counseling	4.23	4.29*	2.44	3.67*	-	-
Counselors	-	-	-	-	-	-
Tutorial program	3.35	3.17*	3.17	3.83	3.85	4.00
Recreational program	2.20	2.97	-	-	-	-

*significant difference: P < 05 between graduates and dropouts.

These individuals were also asked to "rate the (appropriate staff position, such as counselor's) qualifications to provide the service you needed," with the response being on a similar seven-point scale ranging from "1" for extremely good to "7" for extremely bad. Finally, the graduates or dropouts were asked to "rate the pace of the program" on the same seven-point scale from "1," extremely fast to "7," extremely slow.

Table 3.7 presents the average responses to the questions described above. Vocational Training and the Recreational program are tied for the "most useful" component (recall that the lower score, the more useful), with group counseling a very poor last. As was mentioned above, this may have been because group counseling was discontinued in 1972. Also, group counseling is normally an activity associated with the upper-middle-class intelligentsia and may, as it is currently presented, be inappropriate for rural poor families.

As was also mentioned, counselors as individuals were rated quite high, while the counseling-oriented program components were all rated near the bottom.

The "tutorial program" includes the tutoring that adult family members seeking a GED received in the Learning Center, as well as the tutoring of school-age children. In any case, it was rated very low (next to last) by AJC graduates. However, this component was rated relatively higher (third) by dropouts. As might be expected, except for one case (the tutorial program usefulness), dropouts uniformly rated program components less useful, personnel poorer, and programs slower than did graduates. The difference in ratings are significant at the 5 percent level in most cases.

It is interesting to note that the ratings in Table 3.7 are heavily skewed toward the positive side; that is, they are lower than 4.00, which would be a neutral rating. In general, both graduates and dropouts seemed to feel that all program components were helpful, that the personnel were well qualified, and that the pace of the instruction was just about right.

THE ORGANIZATIONAL CLIMATE

Figure 3 shows AJC's organization chart down to (approximately) one level below the division manger level.

Any large organization is composed of a number of individuals, all of whom have their own idiosyncratic needs, goals, and working styles, as well as a number of subunits (departments, teams, and so forth) that also have varying goals, responsibilities, and needs. The degree to which any organization can integrate the various individuals and subunits that make up the body into a cooperative, problem-solving team determines its overall effectiveness.

FIGURE 1

AJC Organization Chart

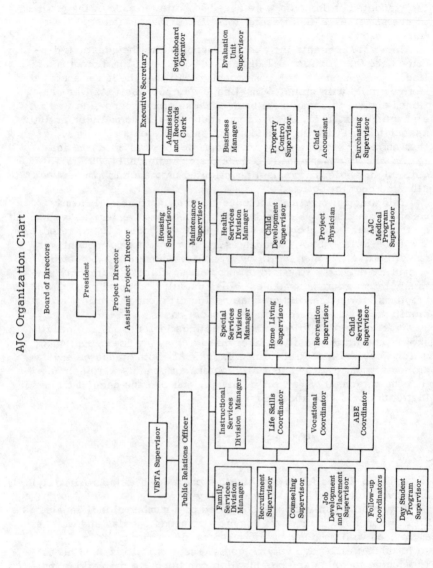

Source: Compiled by the authors.

This section analyzes AJC as a total functioning team, as well as its respective subunits. Hopefully, this analysis will picture clearly the many strengths of AJC, as well as some of its problems, and thus facilitate its further development along healthy organizational lines.

The way a work setting is structured, organized, and administered creates an organizational climate within which the worker functions to seek both satisfaction from his job and to carry out those tasks assigned him by the organization. The Litwin Scale seeks to measure organizational climate by ascertaining the workers' feelings of and perceptions about the surrounding on-the-job environment (Litwin and Stringer 1958). If the organizational climate is structured to fit the motives and needs of the worker, a happy, productive work force will result. If the organizational climate and the workers' motives clash, problems will arise, ranging from low productivity to high job turnover, as staff seek more satisfying work elsewhere.

Nine dimensions of organizational climate are identified on the Litwin Scale. These subscales are: Structure, Responsibility, Risk, Standards, Rewards, Support, Conflict, Warmth, and Identity.

A high score on the Structure subscale means that the person perceives the organization as operating in a highly formal atmosphere with many rules, rigid and strict job definitions, and much red tape, which combine to highly constrain the scope of the individual's freedom within the organization. A low score on Structure, as with the other scales, indicates just the opposite.

A high score on Responsibility indicates that the person sees his job as giving him a lot of individual responsibility. Responsibility is positively related to the need for achievement in the sense that a person with a high need for achievement wants to be able to control the means of attaining his goals and emphasizes the importance of "being your own boss."

A high score on the Warmth scale indicates a friendly work environment. Warmth may be differentiated from support (see below), which is more a feeling of respect for others. Warmth is positively related to the need for affiliation and is not related to the need for achievement or the need for power.

A high support score indicates a perception of the work environment as supportive, reinforcing, and sustaining on a business or professional basis; that is, the kind of support measured by this scale is job-/ or task-related. Support is unrelated to the need for power, and positively related to the need for achievement and the need for affiliation.

A high Reward score indicates that the person is rewarded for good work – it indicates a reliance on the carrot rather than on the stick on the part of management.

A high Conflict score indicates the presence and tolerance of conflict within the organization. Since conflict gives a person a chance to influence others, conflict is positively related to the need for power. An organization high in conflict is an unhappy place for people with a high need for affiliation.

A high score on Performance Standards indicates that management is perceived as setting the standards of job performance as opposed to the individual's establishing personal standards of job quality.

Identity is defined as the extent to which the individual personally identifies with the goals of the workgroup. It is a feeling of belonging to the team as a highly valuable member. Identity is highly related to the need for affiliation, somewhat related to the need for achievement, and unrelated to the need for power.

A high Risk score indicates an environment which emphasizes taking a calculated risk rather than playing it safe, and which gives a feeling of challenge and riskiness in the job. Individuals with high need for achievement characteristically prefer to take moderate risks (that is, those where the subjective probability of success is about 50-50). Risk is positively related to the need for achievement and negatively related to the need for power and the need for affiliation.

In terms of assessing the impact of the climate of the organization upon job performance and satisfaction, organizational climate is closely tied to worker motivation. The nine subscales used to measure organizational climate assess the impact of the managerial atmosphere of the organization upon job performance and job satisfaction. The Litwin Scale aims to identify those aspects of the work environment which satisfy various worker motives. Specifically, the Litwin Scale deals with satisfiers of the need for power, the need for achievement, and the need for affiliation. According to Litwin and Stringer, "all these qualities of motivation have been shown to be important determinants of performance and success in business and government organization" (1968).

Persons with high need for achievement are characterized by a desire to take personal responsibility for solving problems; a desire to set moderate goals and take calculated risks; and a desire for feedback on their effectiveness. They are concerned for success in competition with some standard of excellence.

Persons with a high need for power are chiefly concerned with influencing others, and they seek control of the means of exerting influence.

A high need for affiliation is characterized by the view that warm and friendly relationships with others are the most important values in life, and being isolated and disrespected are the worst things that can happen to a person. In the work arena, the person with a high need for affiliation would tend to perform well in order to be accepted by others, but he would not be particularly motivated by objective standards of performance. Table 3.8 summarizes the relationship between the nine subscales and the power, affiliation, and achievement motives.

Since Litwin and Stringer do not present a scoring system of translating responses on the nine subscales into high or low scores for assessment of motivation, high and low were defined relatively

TABLE 3.8

Correlations of Motivation and Climate Dimensions

Scales (Dimension)	Motivation			Comment
	Power	Affiliation	Achievement	
Structure	+	–	–	This dimension measures perception of formality and constraint in the organization and is empirically quite independent of the other factors. Structure appears to be positively related to the development of power motivation and negatively related to the development of achievement and affiliation motivation.
Responsibility	+	0	+	These dimensions measure the perception of challenge, demand for the work and opportunity for a sense of achievement. The challenge factor appears to be strongly, positively related to the development of achievement motivation, moderately related to the development of power motivation, and unrelated (or negatively related) to the development of affiliation motivation.
Risks	–	–	+w	
Standards	0	–	+w	
Reward	0	+	+	These dimensions measure the emphasis on positive reinforcement rather than punishment for task performance. The reward and support factor appears to be positively related to the development of achievement and affiliation motivation, and generally unrelated to the development of power motivation (except for conflict, which is power-related).
Support	0	+	+	
Conflict	+	–w	+w	
Warmth	0	+	0	These dimensions measure the emphasis on sociability, belonging, and group membership. The social inclusion factor appears to be positively related to the development of affiliation motivation, weakly related to the development of achievement motivation, and unrelated to the development of power motivation.
Identity	0	+	+	

Notes: + : The presence of the dimension is arousing of the motivation.
 – : The presence of the dimension is reductive of the motivation.
 0 : The presence of the dimension has no effect on that motivational pattern.
 +w : The presence of the dimension is positively but weakly correlated with the motivational pattern.
 –w : The presence of the dimension is negatively but weakly correlated with the motivational pattern.

91

based on the overall pattern of responses for the AJC staff. The scores
were trichotomized with scores greater than 2.8 being classified as
"high" and scores lower than 2.6 as "low." Medium scores, those
between 2.8 and 2.6, were ignored in the following calculations,
since Litwin only discusses a dictomous situation. The logic of the
analysis presented below in Table 3.10 is as follows. Having identified
the high and low scores of the AJC staff, their pattern can be compared
to the three configurations given by Litwin and Stringer for the three
motivations, affiliation, power, and achievement. The greater the
correspondence between the AJC staff scores and Litwin's configuration,
the more AJC's organizational climate satisfies that motive. If we make
some assumptions about the nature of AJC and the type of people we
would expect to work there, we can then hypothesize what kind of
an organizational climate would be optimum for AJC. By administering
the Litwin Scale to the AJC staff, we can then see how close AJC
comes to providing the hypothesized optimum environment.

Since AJC is engaged in helping people work, it is very likely to
attract people with high affiliation motivation. If AJC is seen as
exploring the frontiers of "people-work," it could also attract people
with a high need for achievement. The power motivation poses a
dilemma. Generally the need for power and the need for affiliation
are negatively related. A person who has a need to warmly relate to
others is not likely to want to manipulate or control others. However,
AJC is specifically designed to manipulate the client-families, so the
relationship between AJC and the need for power is not clear.

Table 3.9 shows Litwin's configuration for the three motives. Table
3.10 shows the number of matches or mismatches between the scores
shown in Figure 2 (below) and Litwin's configurations. "Medium" scores
and "0" were disregarded in computing the matching. The extent of
match was summed over all three administrations of the Organizational
Climate scale—that is, each value in Table 3.9 could be matched three
times in computing Table 3.10. It is clear from Table 3.10 that the
working climate at AJC is most conducive to the affiliation motive, as
hypothesized. As Litwin suggests, the affiliation and power motives
are negatively related, with the AJC climate being somewhat anti-
thetical to the power motive. This is a very interesting finding, for it
suggests that although AJC practices "people-work" and therefore
provides a work setting that is highly satisfying to the affiliation need,
the antipower climate demonstrated by the test suggests that AJC goes
about its work in a helpful and supportive manner, rather than in a
manipulative (power-seeking) fashion. The absence of an atmosphere
of manipulation would seem to be very important in a rehabilitation
program like AJC, whose very comprehensiveness carries a danger of
"big brother" overtones.

TABLE 3.9

Litwin Subscale Profiles for the Affiliation, Power, and Achievement Motives

Motive	Structure	Responsibility	Reward	Risk	Warmth	Standards	Conflict	Identity
							Subscale	
Affiliation	L	O	H	L	H	L	L	H
Power	H	H	O	L	O	O	H	O
Achievment	L	H	H	H	O	H	L	H

Note: H = positive relationship or high score
 L = negative relationship or low score
 O = no relationship

TABLE 3.10

Correspondence Between AJC Staff Scores and Optium Profiles for
Affiliation, Power, and Achievement Motives

Motive	Matches	Mismatches
Affiliation	14	4
Power	0	7
Achievement	11	7

93

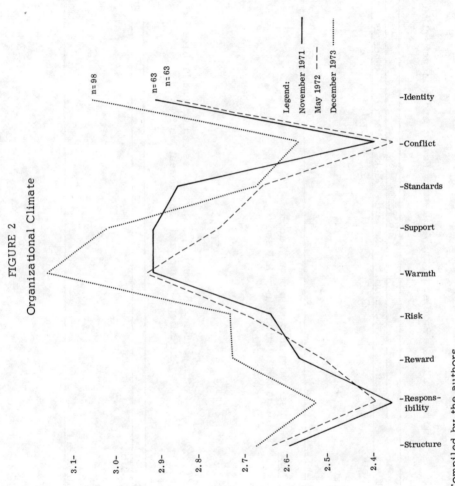

FIGURE 2
Organizational Climate

Legend:
November 1971 ——
May 1972 ————
December 1973 ···········

n=98
n=63
n=63

-Identity
-Conflict
-Standards
-Support
-Warmth
-Risk
-Reward
-Respons-
 ibility
-Structure

3.1-
3.0-
2.9-
2.8-
2.7-
2.6-
2.5-
2.4-

Source: Compiled by the authors.

Figure 2 permits the analysis of change over time in the AJC organizational climate by comparing the subscale profiles at three points in time over a two-year period.

As can be seen in Figure 2, there is little difference on the Structure subscale between the three respective profiles. This would indicate that the staff of AJC perceive the organization as continuously operating within essentially the same organizational parameters. Compared to other organizations studied on the Litwin Scale, AJC falls within a normal range of organizational patterns.

A higher score in Figure 2 on responsibility indicates that the AJC staff came to feel more "like their own boss" and to experience a greater degree of individual on-the-job responsibility than they did initially.

A higher score on Reward indicates that AJC staff perceive themselves as being rewarded more readily for a job well done than punished for poor work. In other words, managerial reward is given more often than is indicated in previous assessments.

The score on the Risk subscale, which measures the sense of riskiness and challenge in the job as opposed to a play-it-safe attitude, is essentially the same in the later as in the earlier profiles.

The Warmth subscale is scored at a much higher level in the last assessment and indicates that the AJC staff came to experience the organization as a friendlier, more pleasureable environment as time passed, and that they came to perceive it as providing a higher level of colleagueship and companionship. Considering the nature of AJC's "people-work," this change is all to the good.

The score on the Support subscale also became higher, and indicates a perception of the work environment as providing a greater degree of mutual support from one's colleagues, as well as an increase in the general helpfulness of those at the managerial level.

A comparison of the scores on the Standards subscale indicates that the individual worker establishes his own personal standards of job quality, letting those standards be determined primarily by top management.

The higher Conflict score in the later assessments indicates a slight trend toward greater tolerance of conflict within AJC and the allowing of influence to be expressed at more levels within the organization.

The last subscale, Identity, is scored slightly higher in the later assessments and suggests that the AJC staff identifies more with the overall goals of the organization and that the individual worker feels more of a sense of belonging to the team as a valued and important member.

In summary, the latest Litwin Scale assessment indicates an overall improvement over earlier measurements along some major organizational climate dimensions, with the greatest degree of change on the dimensions of Responsibility, Reward, Warmth, Support, Conflict, and Identity and less change on Structure, Risk and Performance Standards.

Overall Organizational Climate Based on Interview Data

A number of private interviews were conducted over a three-day period with AJC staff by a special consultant who was an expert in organizational development. The purpose was to discover feelings, attitudes, and work relationships that would clarify and depict the organizational climate more fully than would an attitude questionnaire. It was also believed that interviews would afford an opportunity to analyze the various subunits (such as departments and teams) along similar dimensions, since the climate in any department may be different from that of the organization as a whole. The special consultant's report follows.

The interviewer was impressed with the high degree of dedication, commitment, and family-centered values of the AJC staff. This level of dedication was surprising to the interviewer who has had extensive experience in working with a variety of other poverty-oriented programs and educational instutitions, where frequently the needs of the client were only third or fourth priority and clearly came after staff and organizational needs.

AJC staff at all levels consistently demonstrated an attitude of the "families come first" and that other priorities took second or third when in conflict with the needs of the client-families. This attitude leads to staff working longer hours than one would expect in most organizations and working with the families in a variety of time consuming but necessary and creative ways. When asked, on an anonymous questionnaire, to indicate what they saw as some of the strengths, the staff at all levels frequently wrote such terms as " a great people-oriented program," "genuine concern for others," "a belief that we're improving the life of people and the community—giving a second chance to those who want it," "above all the families are most important," etc. This high level of commitment and dedication was pervasive on the part of many staff throughout all levels of the organizations and helped compensate for other perceived organizational deficiences.

The basic deficiences, as described by AJC staff on the questionnaire and during the interviews, centered in three areas:

(1) a number of staff expressed the belief that there
was not enough opportunity to advance to management levels within the system or to develop increased professional skills for the job at hand,

(2) many staff complained of the "lack of communication" between different parts of the organization as well as the different levels; e.g.,
statements were made such as "executives seem
out of touch with lower-level staff," "directions
come from above without consulting staff," "messages come down but don't seem to go up from those
below," "we aren't sure exactly what others in
AJC are doing," "we're not together on goals for
the families (between departments) because of
poor communication," etc.,

(3) a number of staff feel that there is not enough
reward or appreciation shown by top management
for those who fulfill their responsibilities in an
exceptional and creative way or who clearly work
"beyond-the-call-of-duty"; conversely, this lack
of reward is compounded by the perception that
others who only do a mediocre job and who seldom
"pull-their-load" are not reprimanded or punished.

With respect to (1) above, there is no doubt that internal
organizational advancement has been at a low level since
AJC's inception. This fact of course then leads to a "there's
no place for me to go" feeling on the part of staff who want
to stay with AJC and improve professionally at the same time.
It no doubt has been one of the factors leading to the 7 percent
annual (for 1973) professional turnover rate at AJC.
According to the new Director of Personnel, policies for
internal advancement are in the process of being significantly changed. At least this is true at the policy level.
Whether it is implemented within the organization remains
to be seen.
    The Personnel Director explicitly stated that one of his
major goals was to develop a "job-enrichment" and "career-
planning" program for staff. Thus, rewards for those who
increase their competence on the job will more readily be forth-
coming. These rewards could include advancement within
the organization as well as lateral moves to develop increased professional and managerial skills.
He also described a beginning program for management
training at the supervisory level that would hopefully not
only facilitate the management effectiveness of any unit

within the organization but also lead to higher-level
executive positions for those staff desirous of moving
upward.

The foregoing goals are certainly improvements at the
policy level and if implemented throughout the organization will lead to lower turnover of staff and increased
morale. Of course the effectiveness and thoroughness
of their implementation, as in any organization, is the
critical question that remains to be answered.

With respect to (2) above, this particular problem is almost
universal in contemporary organizations, especially in
those that are growing increasingly more complex and
multifaceted, as in the case of AJC. Part of the problem
was alleviated recently by physically locating staff more
closely together who have linking-roles with the client
families. More changes of this nature would be helpful
as there is increasing evidence that physical proximity,
barring other problems, leads to more frequent and
helpful communication.

The communication difficulties also indicate the increasing
need for the development of team and interteam communication pathways. As the task of any organization grows in
complexity, it requires greater specialization among its
various parts, a greater diversity of roles and functions
and yet at the same time an increased ability to communi-
cate in order that the many functions are integrated, com-
plementary to each other. On the part of the staff it requires
a greater awareness of each others' roles and functions and
an increased ability to convey the most relevant information
in a shorter period of time. Clearly an ongoing program is
needed that regularly allows relevant data to be communicated up and down hierarchical levels and across organizational lines. If this does not occur the end result is an increase in information gaps between staff who ultimately
affect the same client system, and a decrease in the degree
of trust and openness necessary for overall team effectiveness.

With respect to (3) above, a number of staff believe that
whether one does well or poorly on the job is of no real
significance to AJC management. Consequently, those who
do work in an exceptional way only continue to do so out
of dedication to their client-families rather than for the
rewards of the organization. This form of job-satisfaction,
intrinsic to working with the families and experiencing their
appreciation, sustains many AJC staff for some time, but
without organizational reward some have and many will
eventually experience a growing apathy and disillusionment.
This interviewer believes that more executive effort should
be put into developing procedures for noticing and rewarding

the exceptional, competent effort and conversely for
distinguishing between that behavior and those who perform in a half-hearted, mediocre manner.

AJC has a large number of committed, dedicated staff who
place the families and their needs above anything else, more
so, in this interviewer's experience, than is found in most
organizations. That dedication and commitment is its major
strength. Not rewarding such behavior, either by organizational notice or by job advancement, increased pay, etc.,
will ultimately erode and deplete the very resource that
has so far enabled it to fulfill its task so exceptionally
well.

Organizational Climate Within Divisions

AJC staff within every subunit were interviewed an an attempt to
analyze the particular climate within a division and to discover its
individual strengths and problem areas.

An anonymous self-report questionnaire was administered to all
AJC staff in which they were asked to assess the organizational
climate within their respective departments. The comparison of divisions
on this questionnaire is found on Figure 3. Follow-up interviews with
a sample of persons in each area, and the data from the assessment
led to the conclusions that follows.

Family Services. There has been a significant, positive change in the
morale and work attitude of staff in Family Services, partly due to an
increase in staff size from two counselors to six during the eight
months before the assessments, thus enabling the staff to give more
specific attention to family needs. A large part of the change is a
result of the efforts of the new administrator to develop an effective
counseling approach and a clarification of counseling goals. The
department began the process of holding a series of goal-setting
meetings in which an overall philosphy was first discussed and agreed
upon by the staff and then was made operational by explicitly stating
what counseling behaviors would ideally reflect the goals agreed upon.
The administrator regularly involves the counseling staff in these
discussions and, in the authors' opinion, the staff members generally
felt that the end result was a product of the total team effort and not
just of the ideas of the administrator.

The interview results and comments made on the questionnaire by
the counseling staff indicated an increasing feeling that the old
problems of poor communication, poor team effort, and confusion
about counseling goals, were gradually being eliminated. Esprit de corps
was definitely on the upswing and led to such statements by the

FIGURE 3

Team Effectiveness

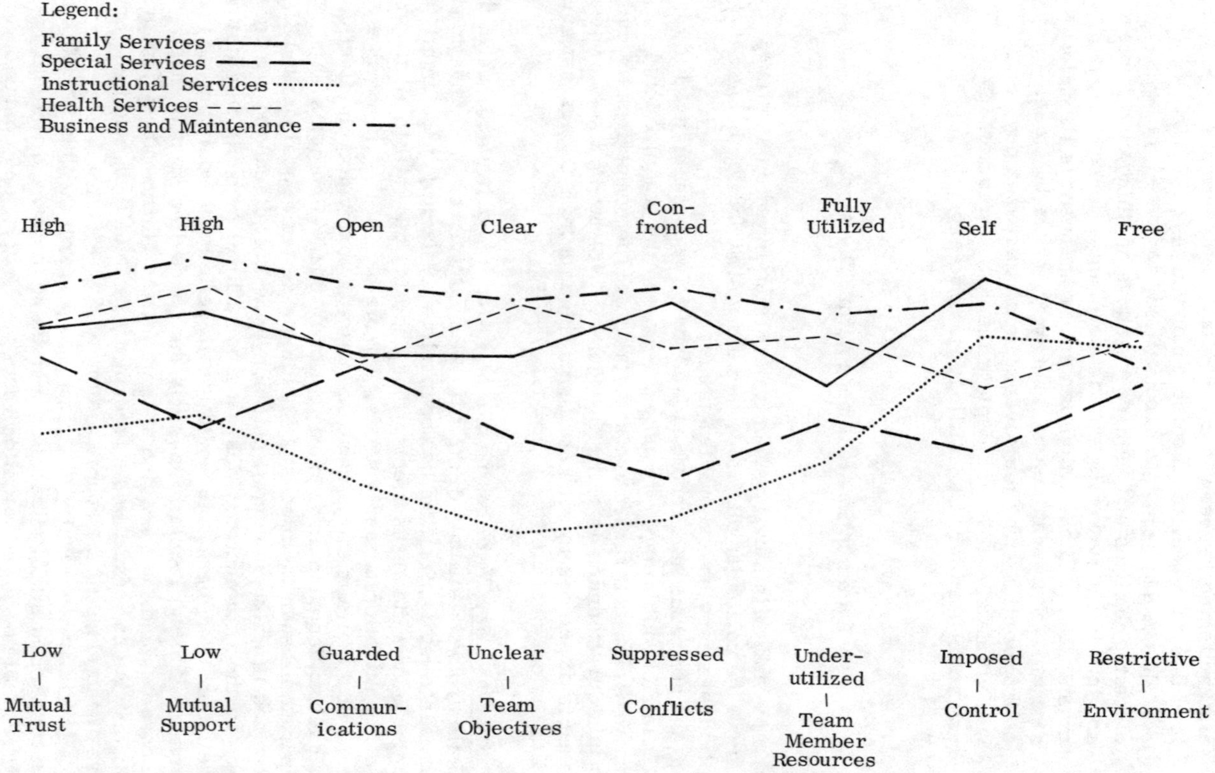

Legend:

Family Services ——————
Special Services ——— ———
Instructional Services ·············
Health Services – – – –
Business and Maintenance —·—·—·

High   High   Open   Clear   Con-   Fully   Self   Free
        —   —   —   fronted   Utilized   —   —
Low   Mutual Guarded   Unclear   —   Under-   Imposed   Restrictive
Mutual Support Commun-   Team   Suppressed utilized   Control   Environment
Trust   ications   Objectives Conflicts   Team
                                                      Member
                                                      Resources

Source: Compiled by the authors.

staff as "we're working well together," "people help each other out," "we have a greater sense of team committment," "there's more co-operation and added support when needed," and "Jack (the administrator) has an open door policy to us on the staff, its much better than before."

Special Services. As the data in Figure 3 indicated, the Special Services division scored somewhat lower on the dimensions of team support, open communication, clarity of team objectives, and use of team resources. These data coincide with the observations of the interviewer.

Special Services is composed of three subunits, Home Living, Child Services, and Recreation. The latter two areas functionally have much in common and work extensively together. Home Living is almost a separate entity with far fewer functional ties to Recreation and Child Services than the latter have to each other. The end result, as evidenced by the data in Figure 3, was a disconnected feeling within the division, coinciding with a lower level of support and trust as well as a lack of unity around the division's goals.

This problem was compounded by the fact that the division manager had not been able to weld the division into a functionally unified team. The manager's approach was a laissez faire management style which allowed each person and each section to operate almost independently. In some settings this approach might be appropriate for management effectiveness, but not where three sections are administratively a part of the same division.

The same laissez faire approach by the manager seemed to contribute to the belief by some in the division that they were "on their own" when they had to influence the system at large in order to garner resources, effect changes, or accomplish other goals. They did not have the feeling that they could count on their division manager to champion their cause effectively or to make their needs and wishes known assertively to higher levels of the organization when necessary. This perception negated a "total" team spirit, since it tended to create an "every man for himself" attitude in getting jobs done, instead of the staff first looking to each other or to their own division for the support needed in the organizational arena.

On the questionnaire, in the area of strengths, staff made such comments as "talented co-workers," "high concern for families," "people help each other out," "a lot of trust with people in my own group," "cooperative atmosphere." These comments would indicate that within subunits there is a positive feeling of working together and helping each other when needed. The problem, as referred to previously, in across unit lines, not within teams. When commenting on the problem areas, such comments as the following were made: "not enough support from higher staff," "physical distance between buildings," "difficulty at arriving at a decision," "lack of active supervisory attention to teams," and "supervisor-staff tensions."

In summary, Special Services is administratively difficult because of the lack of integrated functional responsibilities across the three subunits. At best it would be a difficult situation to weld together, but the dedication and commitment and motivation of everyone in the division (including the administrator) is present, without question. The interviewer was impressed with the motivation of the Special Services staff, with their concern for the client-families, and with their willingness to work hard and creatively to do their job. Either separation into two divisions or much stronger administrative leadership and team building efforts are necessary.

Instructional Services. Instructional Services appeared to be in the greatest difficulty, as was evidenced on the profile of Figure 3. Compared to other departments in AJC, it scored lower on trust, mutual support, communication, team objectives, conflict, and use of team resources, with the lowest scores on team objectives and conflict.

Again, as in the case of Special Services, although worse than the latter, Instructional Services lacked a total sense of organizational unity. This stemmed from personality conflicts, a basic conflict in the theoretical approach to teaching, and inadequate administrative leadership.

In the area of teaching, a continual struggle existed and prevented the team from working together effectively. The conflict in theory had to do with such issues as student-centered versus teacher-centered, and structured versus unstructured classes; emphasis on student-teacher rapport versus a directive, more authoritarian style; and detailed behavioral learning goals outlined for students by the staff versus more spontaneous generation of learning goals as the class develops. Both philosophical positions were represented by two outspoken, assertive individuals who, in the interviewer's judgment, would also have had difficulty working together just on the basis of personality conflict alone. The latter, combined with different approaches to teaching, resulted in lengthy staff meetings and frequent confrontations, intermixed with periods of silent avoidance on the part of those involved.

This basic internal rift within the division led to each staff member working on his own, in his own manner, by himself, without help or observation by others within the division. Thus, particular teaching resources, such as creative ideas, skills, and methods were not shared among the staff and, conversely, poor or inadequate teaching was not evident or observable. This last occurred because anyone who needed or wanted help found it difficult to admit to having problems in the competitive, conflicted atmosphere of the division as a whole.

The communication problem was compounded by less than adequate administrative leadership, both downward within the division, and upward, in representing organizational needs to higher levels of authority. The leadership style was referred to by many as "passive," "laissez faire," "doesn't seem to care," "hard to know where he is," "throws you off guard at times," and so on. This particular management approach certainly did not help a divided and alienated division and probably exacerbated it. In discussions with the administrator the interviewer was impressed with his good intentions, but somehow these were not seen by the staff as being implemented in needed administrative leadership.

The strengths of individual staff members were clearly evident. Most were competent instructors who, as is true for most personnel at AJC, are dedicated to their task beyond what one frequently finds in many organizations. They had a high concern for meeting the needs of their client-families and for giving them the kind of competent training necessary to facilitate their success in the program and in society. Many of them were resourceful and creative in their teaching methods, as they attempted to achieve their respective goals, and here and there some individuals went out of their way to help each other out when called upon or when needed. However, the organizational climate nullified what could have been accomplished if individual talents had been pooled into one unified team.

On the questionnaire, in the area of strengths, such comments were made as "everyone is interested in the good of the students," "a concern for a good program to the families ," "concern for the best possible teaching to the families," "talented and creative teachers," "individuals work hard to make their classes good ones." But these comments were in contrast to those mentioned in the problem areas as "personality conflicts—hard to make decisions," "lack of communication," "lack of openness and agreement," "people on ego trips— become defensive when confronted with problems. . . stay in own little boxes," "people afraid to speak up," "weak leadership—no direction," "conflict in philosophy—all suppressed," and "no one knows what anyone else is doing—everyone in their own cubbyhole."

In summary, Instructional Services was divided on philosophical and theoretical issues as to teaching methods and teaching goals. It was in difficulty as a result of basic personality conflicts among the staff and an administrative leadership style that was too passive to adequately resolve the problems and unify the team.

It would seem that there should have been either changes in staff and leadership or the development of a team-building program that would involve the in-depth use of a competent outside organizational consultant.

Business, Medical and Maintenance. The other three divisions, Business, Medical, and Maintenance all appeared to be doing relatively well, as far as their organizational climate was concerned. Their scores on the team analysis scale of Figure 3 were within a healthy range.

The Medical division had high espirit de corps. Many individuals wrote such phrases as "we work well together," "communication and cooperation is high," and "most of us love our job," whereas the problem area statements had more to do with needing more staff, developing greater technical competence in order to advance, and getting more cross-job training; a few were in the area of needing better communication between people. Based on the assessment data and the interviews it seems clear that the Medical division is a well-functioning part of AJC.

The Business division had had a recent change in administration at the time of the assessment. This change had resulted in negative feelings on the part of some staff since the previous administrator was well liked. However, the new leadership appeared to have handled this issue well and was producing a good, organized unit with acceptable morale. In the realm of strengths the staff made comments such as "a lot of cooperation in our area," "talented and dedicated co-workers," and "the Department Head uses courtesy and controls things in a good manner." Focussing on the problems within the Business division they made comments such as "we don't know enough about each others' jobs," "people not cross-trained enough," or "certain people don't know their job well enough." Thus, the comments, the assessment data, and the interviews would indicate hardly any morale or team problems, but rather concerns around technical competence and role functions. The new administration appeared to be aware of both the latter issues and was attempting to make improvements.

The Maintenance section also was functioning at a relatively healthy team level, without evident internal problems. In the interviews its members expressed a high degree of team spirit and a sense of pleasure with their ability to function well. Their only complaint was in sometimes not getting the information needed from other departments in order to meet the needs of the client-families as quickly as they would like, but they had no complaints as to their own internal climate.

Summary

The authors were impressed with the quality of staff at AJC and their dedication, their commitment to the needs of the client-families and their willingness to go unusually far out of their way to do an exceptional job when such was required. A definite sense of mission and purpose pervades the organization throughout all levels. Many of the staff, without question, attribute a large part of this to the excellent model provided by the project director. Even when some staff felt that the director was somewhat too authoritarian or arbitrary at times, they would interlace this criticism with admiration and respect for his willingness to do everything possible for the client-families and his exceptional commitment and dedication to the purpose of which AJC exists. This was quite a tribute, to say the least. One significant staff member (with extensive experience) who perhaps had the greatest degree of criticism of the project director's tendency toward a paternalistic management approach and his unwillingness to hear criticisms from below, also said that the project director was without question the best and most competent top administrator the staff person had known.

AJC, as evidenced on the Litwin Scale, had the best organizational climate in its history at the time of the last assessment, but improvements in the following important areas are a must if the organization is to continue its growth and succeed in its task:

1. There should be attempts to decrease the number and degree of unilateral, arbitrary decisions by top management and increase, throughout the organization, the opportunities for staff and families to voice their complaints and participate in the decisions that affect them.

2. Greater emphasis should be placed on rewarding those staff members who are doing exceptionally well in their jobs, either by public notice, internal advancement, or increases in pay. Conversely, efforts to identify those who are not performing well should also be made and appropriate action taken.

3. Top conflict-resolution and team-building priority should be given to the internal problems of the Special Services department and, more seriously, those of the Instructional department. Both departments are staffed with many competent individuals with high purpose, whose commitment to the goals of AJC and its client-families is unusual; yet their skills and exceptional resources are not being fully used by the organization as a result of the internal problems previously mentioned.

4. Major emphasis should be given to providing organizational pathways for career planning, cross-job training, and, particularly, for job advancement opportunities within the organization.

5. As the organization grows in its tasks, its complexity, and its necessary specialization, it will continue to function effectively only if major efforts are given to building communication links across divisional lines. This is particularly important since the client-families of AJC are affected and influenced by all aspects of the organization and should, without question, be on the receiving end of an integrated, coordinated effort. Confusion between divisions about purposes, goals, and functions, compounded by an inability to convey to each other the relevant client-family information when necessary, will only undermine the ultimate purposes of AJC. This is not the case now but tendencies and patterns are already present; in most organizations these normally increase into major proportions if not alleviated by continual communication-linking efforts.

FIGURE 4

Geographical Layout of AJC Facilities

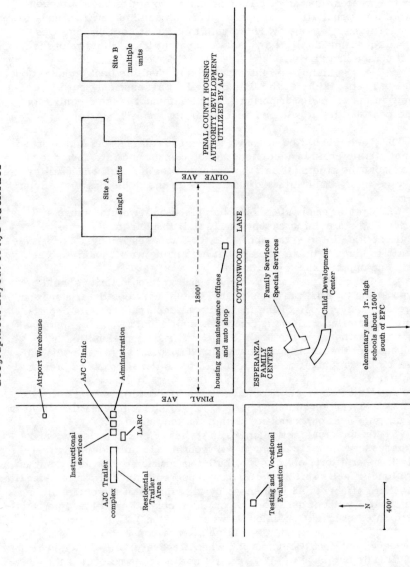

Source: Compiled by the authors.

FACILITIES

AJC utilizes the following facilities in Casa Grande for its
operations. (The area of each facilility is indicated.)
- administrative offices (trailers)—3300 sq. ft.
- AJC Clinic—3600 sq. ft.
- Instructional Services (Learning Center, classrooms, offices)—
  2600 sq. ft.
- ten residential trailers—1000 sq. ft. each
- Esperanza Family Center—17,640 sq. ft.
- PCHA housing development—70 houses averaging about
  1000 sq. ft. each
- downtown warehouse—7500 sq. ft.
- airport warehouse—700 sq. ft.
- testing and vocational evaluation unit—5000 sq. ft.
- Housing and Maintenance offices and auto shop—1000 sq. ft.

The relative geographic locations for each of the above-listed facilities
except the downtown warehouse are shown in Figure 4. Figure 4 is a
rough map of the section of Casa Grande (toward the north side of
the city) where AJC is located. The map illustrates the convenience
of the facilities for AJC families, including the fact that the public
schools attended by AJC children are nearby. The facilities themselves are excellent.

Floor plans for the Esperanza Family Center and the housing,
as well as subdivision maps are contained in SSS 1971, Appendix J.

CHAPTER 4

FAMILY CHARACTERISTICS AT ENTRY

A Brief Profile of AJC Families

This subsection presents a synopsis of data collected through interviews with AJC families at the time they entered the program. The presentation utilizes four hypothetical AJC families, corresponding to the four ethnic groups served by AJC. Each hypothetical family is a composite of the characteristics, at the time of entry, of the ethnic group represented.

The Black Family at AJC. The "typical" Black male head-of-household at AJC had an annual income of only $1724 for the year before he entered AJC. He and his wife were not quite 21 years of age. They had two small children and another one on the way. Since they both went part of the way through the 11th grade before dropping out of school, they were fairly close to getting their GED. They owed a finance company about $250, which they had borrowed to purchase a television set. Despite his low pay, the husband liked his previous job. However, he was pessimistic about improving his life.

The Indian Family at AJC. The average Indian family members at AJC were slightly older than their Black associates. The husband was almost 24 and the wife was 22. They had two small children and a newly-born infant. Their family income for the year before entering AJC was $2493, but they were $840 in debt. The husband, like his Black counterpart, dropped out of school during the 11th grade. His wife, however, had only an 8th grade education. Before coming to AJC, they lived with the husband's parents. The quality of this housing was very low, being far worse than the housing that their Black, Anglo, and Chicano colleagues at AJC had come from. The husband

was very unhappy with his work before coming to AJC. The Indian
family was the most pessimistic of all the families about the future.

The Anglo Family at AJC . The Anglo husband and wife were 29 and 26
years of age, respectively. They both had only 8th grade educations.
Thus, they had been out in the world for some time before coming to
AJC. Despite this fact, their income for the year prior to joining
AJC was only $2529. They had two children and the wife was five months
pregnant with the third. Their housing before coming to AJC was the
best of any of the typical ethnic families, and it was furnished the best.
The husband was reasonably satisfied with his work before coming to
AJC and was neither particularly optimistic nor pessimistic with respect
to his future. However, the wife's optimism exceeded that of all the
other wives.

The Mexican-American Family at AJC . The Mexican-American husband
was relatively unhappy in the job that he had held immediately prior
to coming to AJC. However, this family's total annual income of $2895
was the largest of all the typical families. This family needed more;
they had four children and the wife was six months pregnant. The
Chicano family is older; the husband is 31 and the wife is 28. They
were the poorest-educated, having both dropped out of school in the
6th grade. They had been particularly vulnerable to loan sharks and
were $1666 in debt when they entered AJC. Their house before entering
AJC was rented and in fair condition (second only to the Anglo family's).
The husband was quite optimistic relative to the other husbands. The
wife was nearly neutral where optimism was concerned.

Data Classification

The purpose of the repeated interviewing of AJC participants
was to determine the extent, if any, to which the AJC experience
brought about changes in their lives, their behavior, or their
attitudes. The first 105 families to enter AJC were interviewed three
times: at entry, at the point of departure from AJC, and four or eight
months later. Two interview instruments were used. One was administered to the husband and wife together (if possible), and covered
such items as income, indebtedness, housing, family size, shopping
habits, household furnishings, and vehicle ownership. The other was
administered to the husband and wife separately as individuals, and
covered such items as job history, attitudes, aspirations, and self-
concept.

To facilitate analysis, the data collected in the interviews have
been organized into two parts, independent variables which do not
change (such as ethnicity), or which classify persons into base groups
(such as age or education); and, dependent variables, which measure
those things that could be expected to change as a result of exposure
to AJC. The analysis, then, consists of the detection of changes in

the dependent variables over time, among the subgroups defined
by the independent variables.

The information collected in the three interviews with the first
105 families to go through AJC was analyzed as follows. First, a set
of background characteristics (independent variables) were identified,
which have generally been found to be related to many other variables
in social research. The background characteristics included ethnicity,
age, education, and I.Q. These variables were used to classify the
remaining data into subgroups for the analysis. Thus, the change in
the families' income before and after AJC training was determined for
all families combined, for each of the different ethnic populations,
and for subgroups of different age, education, and I.Q. These comparisons were made on all the variables discussed below. However,
results for the subclassifications are only presented when the .05
level of significance was met. In the following section, "Family
Characteristics at Entry," a profile of the families' social and economic
status at the time they entered AJC is given. The analysis of differences among the subcategories defined by the independent variables
was done by the analysis of variance, t-test, or x^2 test, as appropriate. The next-following section, "Changes in AJC Sample Families,"
looks at the changes in the responses to the items on the question-
naires between entry into and after departure from AJC. In this section
the differences across the three points of time of the interviews—before
AJC, at exit from AJC, and the follow-up several months after exit—were
tested by the analysis of variance, t-test, or x^2 test, as appropriate.
Differences among the subcategories defined by the independent variables
were tested as described above and are only discussed when the statistical significance of the difference reached the .05 level.

The independent variables used in the analysis are ethnicity, age,
education, and score on the Wechsler Adult Intelligence Scale (WAIS).
Age, education, and WAIS were each broken into two categories. The
two categories for age are 28 years or less (AGE-LO) and 29 years or
more (AGE-HI); for education, 8 years or less (ED-LO) and 9 years or
more (ED-HI); and for WAIS, 88 or less (WAIS-LO) and 89 or more
(WAIS-HI). On those items asked of the husband and wife jointly (such
as income or housing), the husband's ethnicity, age, education, and
WAIS score are used, while the individual's values are used on individual items (such as attitudes or self-concept).

The sample of 105 families includes 10 Indian families (9 percent),
21 Anglo families (20 percent), 65 Mexican-American families
(62 percent), and 9 Black families (9 percent). The average age of the
husband is 29.5 years, and that of the wife 27 years. The average
education of both husband and wife is 8.5 years.

The average score on the WAIS is approximately 88. There is a
statistically significant difference (ANOVA, P<.01) among ethnic
groups, with the average scores by group being 83.9 for Indians,
95.4 for Anglos, 85.3 for Mexican-Americans, and 83.1 for Blacks.

The reason for the Anglo average score being so much greater is not
known, but one might speculate that possible cultural bias of the test
is responsible.

Family Characteristics at Entry

The dependent variables used to measure changes in the sample
as a result of the AJC experience were community participation, self-
concept, economic status, attitudes, aspirations, and life styles.
Each of these is measured by a number of items, and its state at entry
is discussed separately below.

Community Participation. The degree to which AJC clients participate
in their communities is measured by the extent of their membership in
local groups, their church attendance, and their registration to vote.
   At entry, only 35 AJC clients belonged to any kind of community
group, including church social groups, nonchurch social groups, unions,
the PTA, the Little League, or other groups. There were no significant
differences among dependent-variable-defined groups on group membership. A group membership scale was calculated as the number of
community groups to which each person belonged. The average value
of this scale at entry was 0.2. The only significant difference (t-test,
$P < .05$) at entry was between the AGE-LO (0.08) and AGE-HI (0.25).
   At entry, 68 percent stated that they attended church. As might
be expected because of the important role played by the Catholic
church in Hispanic culture, the Mexican-Americans had a higher
(ANOVA) $P < .01$) percentage of church attendees (82 percent) than the
Indians (64 percent), the Anglos (40 percent), and the Blacks
(43 percent).
   An important measure of community participation is activity in the
political process. This was measured by voter registration, and it
was found that approximately 25 percent of the AJC clients were registered at time of entry. As would be expected, a significantly larger
proportion of the older persons were registered, but no other significant differences appeared.

Self-Concept. Each member of our sample was asked the question,
"How are you doing now in getting what you want?" In response, 5
percent responded "very well," 32 percent said "pretty well," and
63 percent said "not too well." This pattern of responses was nearly
uniform across groups, indicating a fairly low self-concept. They
were also asked "What do you think your chances are of getting ahead?"
In this case, a certain degree of optimism was shown, in that 22
percent responded "very good," 59 percent "pretty good," and only
19 percent "not too good." Here again, there were no significant
differences between groups.

Another measure of self-concept used in this study is the Hadley Cantril Self-anchoring Scale (Cantril 1965), in which the respondent is asked to indicate on a ten-step "ladder of life" (0 through 9) where he feels he is now, where he feels he was five years ago, and where he thinks he will be in five years (the latter being more a measure of aspirations, which are covered in a later subsection). The average placement on the scale at entry was 3.4 for present, and 2.7 for five years ago. Although there were no significant differences on the placement for the past, the Mexican-Americans and the Blacks placed themselves significantly (ANOVA, $P < .10$) higher for the present than the Indians and the Anglos.

A derivative measure is the individual difference between placement for the present and that for the past, as an indicator of how much the respondent perceives he has come in the recent past. (That is the meaning of the title, "Self-anchoring." That is, the respondent places, or anchors, himself on the ladder "now," and then indicates how far he has come and how far he is going to go by the distance between that placement and the ones for past and future.) The average on this measure (as could be calcualted from the two averages presented above) is 0.7, with no significant differences between groups.

A December 1972 poll by the Gallup organization of 1806 Americans chosen to represent a cross-section of the United States included the same Self-anchoring Scale that was used in this study (Time 1972). The average scores for these individuals were 4.5 for five years ago, 5.4 for the present, and 6.6 for five years from now. The same individuals were also asked to rate the nation as a whole on the same ladder. They saw America at 4.6 five years ago, 4.5 at the present, and 5.2 five years from now.

Economic Status. A number of indicators were examined to determine the economic status of AJC families. These indicators fall in two general classes, financial measures and employment measures. The financial measures included whether the families have a checking or savings account, the amount in the savings account, the families' income, and their indebtedness. The employment measures include two indexes, one of job quality and the other of job satisfaction.

At entry, 9.7 percent of the sample had a checking account, and 17.6 percent had a savings account. The only significant difference on these measures is that the higher percentage of the WAIS-HI group (23 percent) had a checking account than the WAIS-LO group (4 percent).

A selected set of measures of prior annual income before AJC entry are presented in Table 4.1. No significant differences were found between ethnic groups on these measures (using the analysis of variance). The figures in Table 4.1 include an average of $1240 in welfare payments to 13 families. There was a significant difference, as shown in Table 4.2, between AGE-LO and AGE-HI and between WAIS-LO and WAIS-HI on total salary and total income (t-test,

P<.01), but not on per capita income. This would indicate that the higher incomes of the AGE-HI and ED-LO groups are due to their larger families.

The average indebtedness of the 72 AJC families with any debt at all upon entering the program was $1918. Included in this figure are 15 families with an average real estate indebtedness of $2957. The average non-real-estate indebtedness is $1339, excluding those who are free of debt. Table 4.3 presents average number of debts, debt balance, and non-real-estate indebtedness by ethnicity. Table 4.4 presents the same statistics by age, education, and WAIS.

Although the Anglos have a significantly higher number of debts (ANOVA, P<.01), there is no significant difference among ethnic groups with regard to the total unpaid balance. The ED-HI group has significantly fewer debts than the ED-LO group (t-test, P < .05), in addition to a significantly lower debt total (t-test, P < .05). The AGE-LO group has a significantly lower balance (t-test, P < .05) than the AGE-HI group. When real estate debts are excluded, all of the significant differences disappear.

The higher income and indebtedness measures of the older and less-educated groups (AGE-HI and ED-LO) would indicate a greater economic activity among these groups. Perhaps this is a function of family size, but the connection with indebtedness is not clear.

The items comprising the job satisfaction index were not queried at entry. The job quality index (the number of benefits, paid vacation, sick leave, group hospitalization, life insurance, and retirement) obtained on any jobs in the past year) averaged 0.86 for the household heads at entry. There were no significant differences among the ethnic groups at entry.

As far as the items comprising the job quality index are concerned, 11 percent of the husbands had had a job with paid vacation during the year prior to entering AJC, 22 percent had had paid sick leave, 32 percent had all or part of their group hospitalization paid, 10 percent had all or part of their life insurance paid for, and 8 percent had had some kind of retirement plan provided.

Attitudes. The attitudes of the sample members were measured by the Family Scale, which measures feelings of affiliation for the family, Nettler's Alienation Scale (Nettler 1957), and the evaluative aspect of the Semantic Differential on the concepts self, home, family, neighbors, working, communicating, and achieving.

The Family Scale consists of 22 statements about the family or family life, with a five-point scale from "strongly agree" to "strongly disagree." The resulting scale value ranges from a low of 1, indicating negative feelings toward the family and family life, to 5, indicating positive feelings. The average score at entry was 3.3, just slightly toward the positive end of the scale. The AGE-HI group scored 3.4 which is significantly greater (t-test, P<.01) than the 3.2 scored by the AGE-LO group.

TABLE 4.1

Annual Income by Ethnic Background

(dollars)

	Indian	Anglo	Mexican-American	Black	Average
Average total salary	2359	2420	2597	1724	2392
Average total income	2493	2595	2895	1724	2694
Average total per capita income	537	594	577	433	582
Sample size (N = 202)	109	21	63	9	—

TABLE 4.2

Annual Income by Age, Education, and WAIS

(dollars)

	AGE-LO	AGE-HI	ED-LO	ED-HI	WAIS-LO	WAIS-HI
Average total salary	2062	3203	2903	2059	2343	2466
Average total income	2153	3436	3294	2108	2470	2800
Average total per capita income	566	588	612	554	518	631
Sample size	55	41	44	45	46	35

TABLE 4.3

Indebtedness by Ethnic Background

	Indian	Anglo	Mexican-American	Black	Average
Average number of debts	1.6	5.4	3.3	2.4	3.5
Total unpaid balance (dollars)	1199	1370	2354	460	1919
Non-real-estate indebtedness (dollars)	1187	1328	1466	419	1339
Sample size (N=72)	7	14	46	5	—

TABLE 4.4

Indebtedness by Age, Education, and WAIS

	AGE-LO	AGE-HI	ED-LO	ED-HI	WAIS-LO	WAIS-HI
Average number of debts	3.2	3.7	4.0	2.8	3.3	3.7
Total unpaid balance (dollars)	1032	2899	2402	791	2413	1402
Non-real-estate indebtedness (dollars)	867	1805	1287	774	1556	944
Sample size	34	33	32	28	32	23

The Nettler Alienation Scale consists of 15 items, each with either a "yes/no" or an "agree/disagree" response. The resulting scale value is the number of items that the respondent answers in the alienated direction, and ranges from zero, indicating low alienation, to 15, indicating high alienation. The average entry scale value for our sample was 4.4. The WAIS-LO group scored 5.2, which is significantly greater (t-test, P <.05) than the 4.3 scored by the WAIS-HI group. This may be due to the fact that answering some of the items in the scale (such as "do you read Reader's Digest?") in the nonalienated direction requires capabilities beyond those of many members of the WAIS-LO group.

The average score on the three evaluative word pairs (good-bad, ugly-beautiful, and kind-cruel) was calculated, with a range of 1, indicating negative evaluation, to 7, indicating positive evaluation. The average score on the concept "myself" was 5.3 with the Blacks scoring significantly higher (ANOVA, P <.05) than the Indians, the Anglos, and the Mexican-Americans (6.0, as against, 5.0, 5.3, and 5.3, respectively). Perhaps the "Movement" has been felt by the younger Blacks in the Southwest.

On the concept "my home" the average score was 5.3, with no significant differences. On "family life" the average was 5.8, with the older and the less educated scoring significantly (t-tests, P <.05) than the younger (5.8 as against 5.5). On "talking with others" the average was 5.7, with no significant differences. Likewise, the average on "achieving" was 5.7, with no significant differences.

Aspirations. The measurement of the aspiration levels of sample members is based on how much income the respondent would like to make, the ratio of that to how much he thinks he needs, his expectations regarding whether his children will go to college, and his placement on the Hadley Cantril Self-anchoring Scale for the future, relative to that of the present.

The average annual income that the respondents said they would like to make was $8865 at entry, with the Indian and Anglo participants aspiring significantly (ANOVA, P <.05) higher ($11,055 and $10,241) than the Mexican-Americans and Blacks ($8,109 and $8,113). When this aspiration is converted to per capita income, the Indian group joins the Mexican-American and Black with lower wishes of $2,206, $1,782, and $2,175, as compared to $2,781 desired by the Anglos (ANOVA, P <.05). However, when the ratio of how much one would like to make to how much one thinks he needs to make is examined, the Indian group shows the greatest aspiration, with a ratio of 3.7 as against 1.6, 1.5, and 1.2 for the Anglo, Mexican-American, and Black groups, respectively (ANOVA, P <.01). There were no significant differences on these measures between age, education, or WAIS groups.

When asked "Apart from what you would like, do you expect that any of your children will go to college?" 80 percent responded affirmatively, 7 percent were negative, and 13 percent did not know. There were no significant differences among groups.

The average placement on the Hadley Cantril Self-anchoring Scale for "five years from now" was 7.4, which is much higher than that scored by the Gallup sample (6.6) in 1972 (see above). The spread among ethnic groups is fairly wide, from 6.5 for the Indians to 7.5 for the Anglos and Mexican-Americans and 8.2 for the Blacks, and is significant (ANOVA, $P < .05$). The difference between the placement for the present and that for the future, as a measure of how far the respondent feels he is going to go from where he is, averaged 4.1, with the younger members scoring significantly higher (t-test, $P < .05$) than the older, by 4.3 as compared to 3.6. The results of the Hadley Cantril scale administration reveal an amazing degree of optimism among the AJC participants at the time of entry into the program. It is not unlikely that this is an indication that they are vesting a great deal of hope in AJC.

Lifestyle. The life style of the members of our sample was measured by housing status, vehicle ownership, and spending habits.

At the time of entry, 11 percent of the families owned their own home. Significantly greater percentages of the older and the less-educated (x^2, $P < .05$) were homeowners (21 percent and 16 percent, respectively), as would be expected from the findings presented earlier on indebtedness. Another measure of housing status is the number of rooms for each person. The average for our sample was .66, and there were no significant differences by any of the four independent variables.

At least one car or truck was owned by 73 families at entry, with an average value of $669.* No significant differences between groups were found.

The average food expenditure for each person was $22.74 per month at entry, with no significant differences between groups. The average clothing expense was $50.14 a person each year, and again there were no significant differences between groups.

CHANGES IN AJC SAMPLE FAMILIES
A Brief Profile—One and One-half Years Later

This subsection presents a synopsis of follow-up data collected on sample families about six months after leaving AJC, and of the

---

*The value of vehicles is determined by the formula $3900 exp $(-x/4)$, where x is the age of the vehicle in years and "exp" denotes the exponential function. This formula is the result of an analysis of "Blue Book" prices

changes that occured since entering AJC. As was done for the entry
data, four hypothetical families are presented, corresponding to the
four ethnic groups served by AJC. Each is a composite of the follow-
up characteristics of, and changes in, members of the ethnic group
represented.

The Black Family. The Black family seemed to benefit much less from
AJC than any of the others. Their annual income had risen to only
$3877, the lowest of the four types of family, and also the smallest
increase. Their total indebtedness has dropped to about $10 since
AJC. They were slightly more likely to own their own home, but it
was no less crowded than the home they had before coming to AJC.
The quality of the husband's job was only a little higher than that of
the jobs he had had before AJC. The parents' self-concepts had
improved a little, and of the four families, the Black family was the
only one to increase its aspiration levels. The attitudes of this family
had become somewhat less positive, and they had become slightly
more alienated.

The Indian Family. The annual income of the Indian family had
increased to $6760, the highest of the four families. They were a
little more likely to own their own home, and their home, owned or
not, was significantly less crowded at 1.36 rooms for each person
as compared to .54 at entry. The total amount that they owed had decreased to about $150. The quality of the husband's job had increased
greatly. The aspirations of the parents were slightly lower than before
but their self-concepts were much greater. They showed a slight
increase in their levels of alienation, and a shift toward negative
attitudes.

The Anglo Family. The annual income of the Anglo family had risen to
$5974, with a corresponding significant improvement in the quality of
the husband's job. They were much more likely to own their own home,
and hence were in somewhat greater debt than they were at entry. Their
home was much larger, and they were generally much better off
materially than when they started. Their self-concepts had been
bolstered to some degree, but their levels of aspiration had dropped
a little. They evidenced a slight increase in alienation, and a trend
toward less positive attitudes.

The Mexican-American Family. The Chicano family had doubled its
income to almost $6000 per year. They were very likely to own their
own home, which was much larger and less crowded, and they were
correspondingly deeper in debt than they were at entry. The quality
of the husband's new job was much greater than the quality of the
jobs he had held before. There had been a very significant improvement in the self-concepts of both the husband and wife, but no change
in the levels of aspiration. Alienation had increased a little, and
attitudes had shifted toward the negative.

Sample Composition

The members of our sample were interviewed at the time they
entered AJC, when they left AJC, and four and/or eight months
later (follow-up). Not all of the families were interviewed when they
left, or on a follow-up. Some families left AJC without notice, and
many were simply not traceable four or eight months after leaving.
Further, of those followed up some families were interviewed on both
the four- and eight month follow-up; others were interviewed only once. It
was decided that only one follow-up interview would be used for each
family and individual. If both the four- and eight-month interviews
were available (seldom the case), the latter was used. Otherwise,
whatever was available was used.

Of the 105 families and 208 individuals originally included in
our sample, there were 78 families and 141 individuals included in
the follow-up sample. The ethnic composition of the sample at
entry was discussed above. The compositions at the time of leaving
(the exit sample) and four or eight months later (the follow-up sample)
are presented in Table 4.5, indicating very little change in the racial
mix of the sample over time.

Analysis of Changes

The dependent variables—community participation, self-concept,
economic status, attitudes, aspirations, and lifestyle—have
been subjected to extensive analysis in order to determine the extent
to which changes have come about between the time the subjects
entered AJC, the time they left AJC, and the time they were interviewed on either the four-month or eight-month follow-up; this was
done to determine what effects, if any, the exposure of the families
to the AJC experience had on the way they live.

Community Participation. There was no discernable increase in the
extent of group membership over time. Even union membership stayed
constant at about 1.5 percent. PTA membership increased from 3.6
percent to 6.6 percent, but the increase was not significant. The
group membership score went from .20 to .27

Church attendance also showed no increase. At exit, 73 percent
were church attendees, and at follow-up, the level was back to
69 percent, where it had been at entry.

On voter reigstration, however, there was a very significant
increase (x^2, P<.01). While only 25 percent were registered at entry,
43 percent were registered at exit, and 56 percent at follow-up. A

TABLE 4.5

Ethnic Composition at Entry,
Exit, and Follow-up

Ethnic Group	Entry		Exit		Follow-up	
	Number	Percent	Number	Percent	Number	Percent
Indian	10	9.5	7	9.0	5	10.0
Anglo	21	20.0	13	16.7	9	18.0
Mexican-American	65	61.9	51	65.4	31	62.0
Black	9	8.6	7	9.0	5	10.0
Total	105	—	78	—	50	—

significant increase (x^2, P <.05) holds for all of the subgroups defined
by the independent variables, except for the Indian and Black samples.
Even these samples showed dramatic increases—from 10 percent
to 33 percent for the Indians, and from 25 percent to 57 percent
for the Blacks—but, due to their small sizes, the increases were
not statistically significiant. Even the AGE-HI group went from
38 percent to 60 percent.

Self-Concept . In response to the question "How are you doing now
in getting what you want?," there was a significant shift (x^2, P .01)
from entry to exit and follow-up. At entry 63 percent responded "not
too well," while only 26 percent and 33 percent so responded at exit
and follow-up, respectively. The tendency for an increase in the
percentage responding negatively from exit to follow-up holds for
all of the subgroups, and with the exceptions of the AGE-HI, Anglo,
and Black samples, the overall improvement is significant. The AGE-
HI group went from 54 percent to 32 percent to 37 percent; the Anglo
group from 65 percent to 22 percent to 53 percent; and the Black group
from 75 percent to 44 percent to 43 percent.
     The optimism shown at entry in response to the question "What do
you think your chances are of getting ahead?" evidenced no significant
change, either overall or by subgroup. There was a slight but not
significant increase from 19 percent to 23 percent, in the response
"not too good."

The average placement on the Hadley Cantril Self-anchoring scale for "now" increased significantly (ANOVA, $P < .01$) from 3.4 at entry to 4.6 and 4.8 at exit and follow-up respectively. This significant increase held for all subgroups except the Black subgroup, which went from 4.1 to 3.7 to 4.7. The derivative measure of how far the respondent feels he has come in the past five years increased significantly (ANOVA, $P < .01$) from .7 at entry to 1.9 and 2.2 at exit and follow-up. On this measure, only the Anglos and the Blacks among the subgroups showed no significant increase.

Economic Status. The percentage of families having a checking account went from 9.7 percent at entry to 10.5 percent at exit and 22 percent at follow-up. The increase from entry to follow-up is significant (x^2, $P < .05$) but when the exit measurement is included, the increase is not significant. Of the subgroups defined by the independent variables, only the AGE-HI and Mexican-American samples had a significant increase. The percentage having a savings account went from 17.6 percent to 23.1 percent to 40.8 percent, a significant increase (x^2, $P < .05$) which holds for the subgroups defined by age and education and the Mexican-Americans. The average amount in the savings accounts increased, not significantly, from $37.62 at entry to $98.56 at exit and $97.90 at follow-up.

Annualized total salaries and wages increased significantly (t-test, $P < .01$) from $2392 at entry to $5629 at follow-up, an increase of more than 135 percent. This increase was shared by all of the subgroups, but the increase for the Black sample, from $1724 to $3666, was not statistically significant. Total income went from $2694 to $5823, a significant increase (t-test, $P < .05$) shared again by all of the subgroups.

Per capita income showed a similarly dramatic increase from $582 to $1216 per year. This significant increase (t-test, $P < .01$) was shared again by all but the Black group, whose per capita income increased, not significantly, from $527 to $604.

Of those families in our sample having an indebtedness, the average number of debts decreased, not significantly, from 3.5 to 2.8. The total amount of indebtedness increased, not significantly, from $1919 to $3024, and that excluding real estate loans increased, again not significantly, from $1339 to $1796.

All respondents were asked the importance to them of sixteen characteristics of jobs (such as "a job where they judge you only on how you do your work," "a job where you work in an office") and whether that characteristic existed in their present job. A job satisfaction index was computed as the number of characteristics deemed important and found on the present job. This was administered at exit and follow-up only, and increased not significantly from 5.16 to 6.92.

The job quality index (see p. 112, above) showed a significant increase (t-test, $P < .01$) from 0.86 at entry to 2.42 at follow-up. This was shared by all but the Black group which had an insignificant increase from 1.11

to 2.0. Of the items comprising the job quality index, the percentage of job-holders with paid vacation rose significantly (x^2, P <.01) from 11 percent to 64 percent, with sick leave from 22 percent to 45 percent (x^2, P <.01), with group hospitalization from 32 percent to 55 percent (x^2, P <05), with life insurance from 10 percent to 55 percent (x^2, P <.01) and with paid retirement from 8 percent to 25 percent (x^2, P <.05).

Attitudes. There were no significant changes over time in the Family scale. In fact, for the entire sample, there was no change at all, with the average score remaining 3.3. Likewise, for the Nettler Alienation Scale there were no significant changes. For the whole sample, the alienation score went from 4.9 to 5.0, indicating a slight but not significant increase in alienation.

Table 4.6 presents the changes in the seven Sematic Differential concepts over time, with the associated significance level of the change. With the exception of the concept, "my home," all went significantly in the opposite direction from what would have been expected from the objectives of the AJC program. That is, all of the concepts were those which are supposed to be highly evaluated in the "mainstream of American life," which is basic, at least, to the early objectives of AJC. On the other hand, this finding along with that on the Nettler Alienation Scale may indicate a more realistic attitude developing over time among the members of the sample.

Aspirations. Only 13 responses were obtained at follow-up by the field interview team to the question "How much annual income would you like to make?" These 13 respondents, however, evidenced a sharp increase from $8865 per year to $17,385 (t-test, P <.01). The increase is not quite as dramatic when stated in terms of per capita income ($2077 to $3565), but is still a very significant change (t-test, P <.01). The ratio of how much they would like to make to how much they think they need to make rose insignificantly from 1.7 to 2.4 (only 11 responses were obtained at follow-up for both of the two items included in this ratio).

TABLE 4.6

Semantic Differential Averages

Concept	Entry	Exit	Follow-up	Significance Level[*]
Myself	5.3	5.0	5.0	.01
My Home	5.3	5.4	5.4	not significant
Family life	5.8	5.7	5.5	.05
Neighbors	5.4	5.0	5.0	.01
Working	5.6	5.4	5.3	.05
Talking with others	5.7	5.4	5.3	.01
Achieving	5.7	5.4	5.2	.01

[*]ANOVA, P < "Significance level"

The percentage of the respondents expecting their children to go to college decreased significantly (x^2, P<.01), from 80 percent from entry to follow-up, with the corresponding increase in "Don't knows" from 13 percent to 32 percent.

The AJC experience did not change the average placement for "five years from now" on the Hadley Cantril Self-anchoring scale, which remained at 7.4. However, since the placement for the present increased significantly (see "Self-Concept" above), the difference between present and future (from 4.1 to 2.6) was also significant (t-test, P<.01) statistically. However, it is doubtful that this difference has any bearing on aspiration levels, but is simply a reflection of an improved present self-concept.

Lifestyle. The percentage of home ownership among the families in the sample increased significantly (x^2, P <.01) from 11 percent at entry to 38 percent at follow-up, a degree of increase that was shared generally by all of the subgroups. Also, average dwelling size increased significantly (t-test, P <.01), as measured in number of rooms for each person, from .66 to .96. This increase in dwelling size was not shared by the Blacks in the sample, who went from .70 to .72 rooms per person.

The average value of cars and trucks owned by the families increased not significantly, from $669 to $870 between entry and follow-up, with the percentage of families having a motor vehicle remaining at about 70 percent. Among the subgroups as defined by the independent variables, only the lower-educated (at entry) increased significantly (t-test, P<.05) on motor vehicle value, and that was from $579 to $1164.

Average food expense for each person remained nearly constant at between $22 and $23 per person per month. This statistic tells nothing about the composition of the food purchased. The Home Living training component of AJC was supposed to teach the families how to eat better for less money, so that the constant expenditure on a monthly basis may be due to the counter balancing effects of buying more and better at a lower unit cost.

ANALYSIS OF DROPOUTS

AJC's dropout rate has been a concern to the program's management and the evaluation research team from the beginning. Out of the 105-family study sample, 39 families dropped out. Two were later readmitted for a net dropout rate of 37 out of 105, or 35 percent. This dropout rate has steadily increased to about 50 percent, where it remains today.

Analysis of Study Sample Dropouts

An extensive analysis was performed on the study sample data from entry interviews to attempt to arrive at a method of predicting likely dropouts. The dropout population was compared with the graduate population utilizing the following as independent variables:

- early or late arrival
- ethnic background
- average age of husband and wife
- average education level of husband and wife
- whether the family rents, owns, or lives with relatives
- years of residence in Pinal County
- value of possessions
- pattern of use of medical services
- amount of debts
- annual income
- difference in age between husband and wife
- education level of husband only
- education level of wife only
- difference in education level between husband and wife
- number of persons in each room
- housing quality
- insurance coverage
- per capita spendable income
- age of husband
- car ownership
- whether or not car is insured
- whether or not the family had a checking account
- whether or not the family had a savings account

In no instance was there a statistically significant difference; that is, it is impossible to predict, by examining the variables listed above, whether or not a family is a high or low dropout risk.

However, in two of the above-listed cases, some interesting although not statistically significant patterns emerged. These two cases are displayed in Tables 4.7 and 4.8. Table 4.7 indicates that older families are more likely to complete training. Table 4.8 reveals that Anglo families varied from the two to one ratios of graduates to drop-outs which were demonstrated by the other ethnic groups. Tables 4.7 and 4.8 provide some evidence that young Anglo families are a poor risk to complete their training at AJC.

TABLE 4.7

Analysis of Dropouts by Age

Age	Graduates	Dropouts
under 21	11	13
21-29	31	17
over 29	24	9

TABLE 4.8

Analysis of Dropouts by Ethnic Background

Ethnic Background	Graduates	Dropouts
Indian	7	3
Anglo	9	12
Mexican-American	44	21
Black	6	3

Analysis of Recent Terminations

The files of 50 of the 53 AJC families who terminated (AJC uses the word "termination" instead of "dropout") in 1973 were thoroughly examined to determine the reasons for dropping out, whether the termination was voluntary or involuntary, whether the exposure to AJC had clearly helped, and the length of time in the program. Table 4.9 presents the results of this examination. These findings are in nearly total disagreement with those implied in an earlier evaluation of AJC (Amex, 1973, p. 37) which stated that "a large number left the program following domestic differences." Our examination indicates that only 22 percent indicated that marital problems caused, or were even significantly involved in, the termination. Further, fewer than 50 percent of those (10 percent of the sample) evidenced no prior serious marital problems.

Amex further states that a "key factor [in terminations] appears to be the concept of applying middle-class values focused on the male-female joint-decision Anglo-oriented culture." We do not dispute that middle-class values are applied at AJC. Further, it is well established that the imposition of such values upon lower-class, more traditional cultures causes some disruption in marital situations (Stephenson 1968, pp. 160-72). Middle-class values, or more accurately, middle-class lifestyles, call for a much greater participation of the wife in the decision-making process. However, our findings as presented in Table 4.9 indicate that nay AJC-induced marital discord played a minor role in causing AJC terminations in 1973. For example, discipline (rules, timeliness, and so on) resulted in the largest number of terminees. Gratification delay (a certain contributor to terminations involving such reasons as financial problems, training too slow, or found other job) led to even more terminations.

It should be also pointed out that, in general, these "middle-class" values such as deferred gratification, discipline, and so forth, would be derelict in its job training responsibilities if it did not attempt to teach these values to its clients.

Amex (1973) goes on to state that the terminations "occured between the first and fourth month after enrollment." Our examination revealed that termination occured between the month of enrollment and eleven months later, with a mean length of time at AJC of 4.3 months, and a median of four months.

TABLE 4.9

Analysis of Reasons for Terminations and Length of Time Dropout Families Stay at AJC

Reason	Voluntary AJC-helped[a] number	percent	Voluntary Other[b] number	percent	Involuntary AJC-helped number	percent	Involuntary Other number	percent	Time at AJC (months) 0	1	2	3	4	5	6	7	8	9	11	Average Time at AJC
Rules, discipline, drinking, absenteeism	1	20	4	10	5	100	10	20	-	-	2	1	1	1	-	2	2	1	-	5.5
Disappeared, no reason given, or not ascertainable from file	-	-	7	18	-	-	7	14	2	1	-	2	-	2	-	-	-	-	-	2.4
Financial problems	1	20	4	10	-	-	5	10	-	1	-	-	2	1	1	-	-	-	-	5.0
Training inadequate, too slow	1	20	4	10	-	-	5	10	-	2	-	1	2	-	-	-	-	-	-	3.6
Marital, no preexisting problems apparent	2	40	3	8	-	-	5	10	-	-	2	-	1	2	-	-	-	-	-	6.4
Marital, preexisting problems apparent	-	-	6	15	-	-	6	12	-	-	1	-	-	2	-	-	-	1	1	3.2
Found Job	-	-	6	15	-	-	6	12	-	1	3	1	1	-	-	-	-	-	-	3.7
Other[c]	-	-	6	15	-	-	6	12	1	1	-	2	1	-	1	-	-	-	-	4.0
Total	5	-	40	-	5	50	-	-	3	4	7	6	5	13	2	5	2	2	1	4.3

[a] Indication in file that the family derived some benefit from its stay at AJC.

[b] No indication in file that AJC helped.

[c] Includes family problems (nonmarital), never really got started at AJC, medical reasons, and homesickness.

127

THE AJC FINANCIAL SYSTEM

AJC has, during the period covered by this study, received financial support from a variety of sources. The major funding agencies have been the Office of Economic Opportunity (OEO)/Department of Labor (DOL) combination, the Rehabilitative Services Administration (RSA), the Public Health Service, the Department of Housing and Urban Development (HUD), and the Ford Foundation. Most of AJC's funds have been earmarked for specific use; for example, the RSA Initial Staffing Grant funds were specifically for salaries. AJC's financial system was designed to accommodate this multiplicity of funding sources and the earmarking of the various funds for specific uses. The main components of AJC's financial system are the General Fund, from which AJC's day-to-day operating expenses are drawn, and the funding sources accounts, from which the General Fund is periodically replenished. Funds from the AJC General Fund are utilized for the purchase of fixed assets and for covering recurring costs. Expenditures are then analyzed at the end of each month to determine the amounts by which the general fund is to be reimbursed from each of the funding sources. Based on this analysis, money is transferred from the various grant accounts to the AJC General Fund to cover the next month's business activities. Funds from the various grantors are earmarked for specific use; hence, the monthly amounts that can be transferred from each account into the General Fund depends on the types of expenditures made during that month. For example, in July 1970 approximately $54,000 was paid out of the General Fund toward the purchase of trailers for AJC offices and facilities. At the end of the month, RSA's construction grant account was tapped for $27,000, which replaced half of the trailer cost paid out of the General Fund. The other $27,000 came from an account set up with Ford Foundation funds specifically earmarked as matching funds for the RSA grant.

SUMMARY OF AJC GRANTS AND CONTRACTS

This section presents data on the major grants and contracts received by AJC between May 1, 1968 and December 31, 1973. Subsections describing the grants are presented below. The order of these subsections follows the chronological order of the announcements of the grants.

Ford Foundation Initial Planning Grant. Two separate grants were awarded to AJC by the Ford Foundation. The first, a planning grant of $38,000, was announced on May 1, 1968. A portion of this grant was utilized as matching funds for a "program planning and startup" grant, described in the next subsection, from the Arizona Division of Vocational Rehabilitation (DVR).
AJC spent approximately $23,500 of the first Ford Foundation grant during the first fiscal year of its operation, July 1, 1968 to June 30, 1969. In March, 1970, AJC began utilizing funds from the second (larger) Ford grant (see below).

Arizona Department of Vocational Rehabilitation(DVR). In July 1968, DVR awarded AJC a grant of $33,000 for program planning and startup. This amount was matched with $11,000 from the Ford initial planning grant. Subsequent increases in the DVR grant amounted to a total of around $59,000; hence, AJC received approximately $92,000 from DVR during its first one and one-half years of operation.

RSA Initial Staffing Grant. The funds from this grant, announced in June 1969, were earmarked for staff salaries during the startup period. The original grant period was from January 1, 1970 to March 31, 1974. The first phase was 15 months in duration, covering the period from January 1, 1970 to March 31, 1971. The remainder of the grant period was to be made up of three additional 12-month phases. The grant provisions required that nongovernmental matching funds be available to AJC. During the first phase, the ratio of federal to nonfederal funds was 75:25. The federal to nonfederal fund ratios for phases two, three, and four were 60:40, 45:55, and 30:70, respectively. The federal to nonfederal ratio was to be approximately 52:48 for the entire 51-month period.
The total of federal funds released to AJC during the first phase of this grant was $127,191. This was to be matched by $42,397 of Ford Foundation funds.
AJC underran this $127,191 initial phase grant by $30,532 (and consequently there was an underrun on the budgeted matching Ford Foundation funds amounting to $10,177). The total federal commitment for the second phase was $76,791, of which $46,259 was new money,

with the remainder being made up from the underrun on the initial
phase. This amount, however, was less than AJC had expected.
Consequently, AJC requested that the Ford matching funds be increased
for phase II in order to make up the perceived deficit. Ford granted the
request, approving a total of $84,207 as matching funds for phase II.
As a result, the actual federal to nonfederal fund ratio for phase II
was 52.3:47.7. In phase III, the planned federal to nonfederal fund
ratio of 45:55 was approximately adhered to, with $98,670 of federal
money and $122,437 of Ford funds being expended.

   Although phase IV was scheduled to begin on April 1, 1973, AJC
requested that it be delayed until July 1, 1973, for two reasons. First,
a grant from OEO's Migrant Branch was announced late in March 1973.
This third OEO grant covered the salaries of those staff members who
had previously been paid out of Initial Staffing Grant funds. The period
of coverage under that OEO grant was from April 1, 1973 to June 30, 1973.
Second, as of March 31, 1973, the Ford Foundation grant, from which
the matching funds for phase IV were to be obtained, was all used up.
Ford had pledged additional support beginning in fiscal year 1974, so
new money for matching funds would not be available until July 1, 1973.

RSA Construction Grant. Funds from this grant were earmarked for a
"rehabilitation facility." The grant was contingent upon AJC's obtaining
nonfederal matching funds on 50:50 basis. Ford Foundation funds were
utilized to fulfill the matching fund requirement. AJC purchased 20
large trailers with the construction grant funds. These trailers were
utilized for a number of AJC operation facilities: offices, conference
rooms, places of instruction, medical facilities, and housing for
ten families. The fact that RSA allowed AJC to purchase mobile facilities with the grant funds was a "first," in that earlier RSA construction grants had all been for permanent facilities.

   This particular grant of $75,000 in federal funds, and the $75,000
in matching funds drawn from AJC's Ford Foundation money, was all
spent. The 20 trailers for which the grant was earmarked are now the
property of AJC.

Ford Foundation Grants. On September 3, 1969, the Ford Foundation
granted AJC $887,834 to be utilized over a three-year period. This
grant was originally contingent on the approval of federal grants to
AJC totaling $5.5 million. Consequently, release of Ford funds was
held up until AJC received what the Ford Foundation regarded as
sufficient federal funds to begin operation. The OEO grant, described
below, provided the amount which allowed AJC to utilize the initial
portion of Ford grant money.

   At the end of the initial grant period, Ford continued its support
of AJC by providing an additional $300,000, to be used in fiscal year
1974.

The Ford Foundation grant is designed to provide AJC with a large pool of private funds. The existence of such a pool has allowed AJC to apply for federal grants which require matching funds from nonfederal sources. The Ford grant also has allowed AJC some flexibility in its program design, in that certain items which are "unallowable" under the terms of various federal grants can be covered with funds from the Ford grant.

The variety of uses that AJC has made of the Ford money is illustrated by the data presented in Table 5.1. The amount earmarked as matching funds for various grants was $671,098, or 56 percent. The remainder, $516,736, was utilized for program components not covered by federal grants.

The utilization of Ford funds which were not earmarked as matching money for federal grants is interesting, and hence worth discussing in more detail. These categories include the following:

1. OEO/DOL support. Although the terms of the OEO/DOL grants did not require matching funds, AJC established this account to pay for items that are unallowable under the OEO grant, such as medical expenses (prior to AJC's Public Health Service grant), staff salaries for special services, and maintenance expenses.

2. Arizona Ecumenical Council contributions. AJC contributed $60,000 from the Ford Foundation grant to the Arizona Ecumenical Council (AEC) (the corporate entity which is now AJC was a "spinoff" of AEC, Inc.—AEC was the original grantee for funds to start up the project until AJC was able to establish its tax-exempt status). This "contribution" is actually an outstanding example of resource mobilization. AEC has, in turn, contributed $60,000 to the Arizona DVR. This contribution has enabled DVR to obtain an additional $240,000 in federal funds. The $300,000 that DVR found itself richer by was used to purchase various services from AJC; to provide some of the client families' stipend money through DVR "maintenance"; to reimburse AJC clients for tuition expenses at Central Arizona College and elsewhere; to provide transportation for AJC clients to attend classes or vocational training courses; and to purchase medical services, dentures, eyeglasses, and other similar items.

3. Medical (General). These funds were used to pay for AJC client-families' medical expenses not covered by DVR basic support, prior to AJC's being awarded its medical grant.

4. Salaries. After Dr. Louis Y. Nau resigned as president of AJC, Inc. and director of AJC's Pinal County Project, Mr. Goodman was appointed project director and Mr. Bellrichard was hired as president of AJC. This management change essentially created a new high-level staff member, in that Dr. Nau had previously held both positions. This additional staff member was not covered under any existing grants, so Ford gave its permission to utilize funds from its grant to pay Mr. Bellrichard's salary.

TABLE 5.1

Allocations of Ford Foundation Grant
Funds by Utilization and Time
(dollars)

Utilization	April 1, 1970 to March 31, 1971	April 1, 1971 to March 31, 1972	April 1, 1972 to June 30, 1973	July 1, 1973 to Nov. 30, 1973	Projected Dec. 1, 1973 to June 30, 1974	Total
Support of OEO/DOL grants	56,286	118,415	115,367	220	131,448	421,736
Matching funds – RSA Construction Grant (trailers)	75,000	-	-	-	-	75,000
Matching funds – RSA Facility Improvement Grant	-	-	3,333	1,330	2,003	6,666
Matching funds – RSA Initial Staffing Grant	32,220	84,206	122,437	57,998	106,227	403,078
Matching funds – HUD Neighborhood Facility Grant	151,174	20,128	-	-	-	171,302
Matching funds – HUD Grant for Supplemental funds for neighborhood facility	-	-	14,268	784	-	15,052
Arizona Ecumenical Council contribution; seed money for DVR Basic Services Contract support	20,000	20,000	20,000	-	-	60,000
Medical – general	-	15,000	-	-	-	15,000
Salaries	-	-	20,000	-	-	20,000
Totals	334,680	257,749	295,405	60,322	239,678	1,187,834

HUD Neighborhood Facility (Esperanza Family Center) Contract. The
Department of Housing and Urban Development granted the City of
Casa Grande a total amount of $403,958 for the construction of a
neighborhood facility. AJC was instrumental in the acquisition of
this grant, which required matching funds of $201,979 (a federal to
nonfederal ratio of 66.66/33.33). The required matching amount
was made up of $171,302 of AJC's Ford money, $10,583 from AJC
corporate funds, and $20,094 worth of in-kind services provided by
the city of Casa Grande. The latter component, work on the parking
lot, included paving it and doing other miscellaneous work related
to drainage of its entryway. Management of the construction and
operation of this facility was carried out by AJC under contract to
the grantee, the city of Casa Grande.

HUD later provided approximately $30,000 in supplemental funds
for landscaping the family center, which was matched (under the
same ratio as the original grant) by $15,052 of Ford money.

OEO/DOL Grants . The original OEO grant of $550,000 was the key
to the start of AJC's operations. The RSA grants had been approved,
but could not be utilized without the Ford Foundation money. The
Ford Foundation grant, in turn, depended on additional federal funds.
The OEO grant released the Ford funds, which, in turn, allowed utilization of the RSA and HUD grants.

The period over which the first OEO grant was in effect ran from
May 1, 1970 to July 31, 1971. AJC actually spent $485,712 of the first
OEO grant, for an underrun of $64,288.

The second OEO grant (for $992,440) went into effect August 1, 1971.
The grant period was from that date to July 31, 1973. During the year
ending July 31, 1972, approximately $647,100 was used for operating
AJC programs. AJC's original grant request to OEO stated that, during
the second year ending July 31, 1973, the balance of the grant was to
be used exclusively as stipends to pay for living expenses of AJC
families. However, because of financial problems, AJC requested,
and was granted by OEO, permission to use the remaining funds in the
same manner as in the past, that is, for general use. Consequently,
the OEO funds were almost completely exhausted by the end of
February 1973.

The two OEO grants referred to above were awarded to AJC by the
Office of Program Development (OPD). OEO underwent a reorganization
early in fiscal year 1973, and OPD was eliminated. The responsibility
for administering AJC's grant was then moved to the Office of Operations'
Special Program Branch. The premature exhaustion of OEO grant funds
in February 1973 created a financial crisis at AJC, which OEO was able
to ease with a grant of $290,000 from the Office of Operations' Migrant
Branch. At the time when this third OEO grant was awarded, AJC had
prepared plans to wind down its operations; thus, OEO again saved
AJC from having to close.

The Migrant Branch subsequently granted AJC an additional
$460,000 to cover the first eight months of fiscal year 1974. During

this current grant period, the Migrant Branch was moved from OEO to DOL's Manpower Administration and AJC came under the administration of the DOL.

Arizona Department of Health . Early in 1971, a grant of $8,616 was awarded to AJC to provide temporary health services to families. As of June 30, 1971, this grant had been used up.

The Arizona Department of Health (ASDH) subsequently awarded AJC a $154,035 one-year grant, effective July 1, 1971. This grant provided for comprehensive health services to AJC family members, and to about 700 additional medically needy persons in western and central Pinal County.

Health Services and Mental Health Administration (HSMHA) . In July 1972 AJC received a $295,446 grant from the Migrant Health Service (MHS) under HSMHA. The grant funds have been used to continue the delivery of medical services to AJC families and other migrant and seasonal farm workers in Pinal County. This grant established AJC as one of HSMHA/MHS's medical centers.

HSMHA continued its support of AJC's medical operations with $304,000 for fiscal year 1974. This latest grant was recently amended to allow AJC to pay hospitalization costs for the Medical department's target population (migrant and seasonal farm workers in Pinal County). AJC's Medical department thus becomes the first of what will eventually be seven different experiments in providing hospital as well as out-patient medical services to migrant and seasonal farm workers.

Facilities Improvement Grant. On June 30, 1972, RSA awarded a "Facilities Improvement Grant" to AJC. The $30,000 in federal funds were matched by $3,333 in Ford money to comply with the required federal to nonfederal ratio of 90:10. This grant was utilized in fiscal year 1973 for salaries in the areas of job placement, housing, recruiting, and record-keeping. This grant was continued at the same level for fiscal year 1974.

Welfare Recipients' Purchased Services Contract . The Arizona Department of Economic Security contracted with AJC to provide certain services to Arizona welfare recipients. The beneficiaries of these services were families with "solo parent" female heads-of-household or families whose male head-of-household was disabled. The people served under this contract were generally ineligible for the AJC residential training program, and hence were termed "day students" by the AJC staff. AJC provided such services as vocational evaluation, counseling, vocational training, job development and placement, and transportation. As a result of this contract, AJC was able to set up its own vocational evaluation facility. The University of Arizona, under a $46,000 sub-contract, provided vocational evaluation specialists to operate the facility.

The contract period ran from January 1, 1973 to November 30, 1973. Because AJC was dependent on DVR counselors to refer clients to the program, and because these counselors were reluctant to commit their clients to the program on a long-range basis, AJC was able to utilize only $122,000 of the total available amount of $350,000.

Family Planning and Child Care Grants. OEO's Migrant Branch, before it was moved to DOL, transferred $59,509 in grant funds from the Migrant Opportunities Program to AJC's Medical department. The purpose of the grant was to provide family planning counseling and child care training services in the field (in the sociological sense, not the agricultural sense) to migrant and seasonal farm workers in Maricopa County.

A Summary of AJC Grant Funding. Table 5.2 summarizes the important features of the grants described in the previous section; it is useful for comparing startup funding profiles with those of similar or replicated projects. The total also reveals that AJC failed to meet the original contingency of its Ford Foundation grant, which was to obtain $5.5 million in federal grants over the three-year period in which the first Ford grant was in effect.

OTHER INCOME

AJC receives a certain income from its operations. A sizeable portion of this "other income" overlaps that of the DVR client services contract shown in Table 5.2. As of the end of December 1973, the cumulative amounts from various sources were as follows:

Source	Amount (in thousands of dollars)
Rent from residential trailers	23.4
Interest on Ford grant funds	13.5
Insurance settlement	0.7
Donations	1.5
Honorariums	0.6
Income from DVR:	
developmental education	97.5
tuition payments	129.8
hospital refunds	1.6
medical refunds	3.7
terminee unused maintenance	3.3
Total	275.6

The rental income is derived from the ten client families who occupy the ten residential trailers. AJC deposits advances from the Ford Foundation into savings accounts, which explains the "interest" income above. The insurance settlement income item was the result of AJC's filing a claim for storm damage to a large refrigerator which was excess federal government property. The federal government advised

TABLE 5.2

Summary of Major Grants and Contracts

Grantor	Purpose	Amount
May 1968 Ford Foundation	planning	$38,000
July 1968 Arizona Department of Vocational Rehabilitation	program planning and start-up	$33,000 – $59,000 over the following one and one-half years
June 1969 Rehabilitative Services Administration	initial staffing	Phase I : $96,659 Phase II : $76,791 Phase III: $98,670 Phase IV : $70,378
June 1967 Rehabilitative Services Administration	construction	$75,000
September 1969 Ford Foundation	matching funds for federal grants	Fiscal year 1971-73: $887,834 Fiscal year 1974: $300,000
November 1969 Department of Housing and Urban Development	construction of neighborhood facility	$403,958 and approximately $30,000 in supplemental funds
March 1970 Office of Economic Opportunity	general operating expenses	$485,712
July 1, 1970 Arizona Department of Vocational Rehabilitation	client services	Approximately $570,000 in service fees over the first three and one-half years
August 1971 Office of Economic Opportunity	general operating expenses	$992,440
July 1971 Arizona State Department of Health	comprehensive health services	$154,035
June 30, 1972 Rehabilitative services Administration	facilities improvement	First year: $30,000 Second year: $30,000
July 1, 1972 Health Services and Mental Health Administration, Migrant Health Division	comprehensive health services	Fiscal year 1973: $285,446 Fiscal year 1974: $304,000
January 1, 1973 Arizona Department of Economic Security	services to Arizona welfare recipients	$122,000 over a one-year period
March 1, 1973 Office of Economic Opportunity/ Department of Labor Migrant Branch	economic upgrading of migrant and seasonal farmworkers	March-June 1973: $290,000 July 1973-February 1974: $460,000
July 1, 1973 Office of Economic Opportunity/ Department of Labor Migrant Branch	family planning and child care services	$59,509

Note: Total of state and federal grants and contracts: $4,726,598
      Total of all grants and contracts: $5,952,432

that AJC could keep the amount paid by the insurance company.
Donations have been received from various businesses and individuals.
AJC staff members who receive honorariums for speaking appearances
donate the money to AJC. the "DVR developmental education" item
above is the amount of money that DVR pays AJC for training DVR clients
(AJC family members) in the AJC facilities utilizing AJC staff members;
AJC refers to this as "in-house" training. DVR also reimburses AJC
for tuition which AJC pays to outside organizations, primarily Central
Arizona College, for training courses utilized by various AJC family
members. Finally, if AJC is refunded money which it has paid in
behalf of its clients, DVR allows AJC to keep these refunds. (The
refunds are small, so that DVR's cost in processing them would exceed
the amount.) This is also true for unused maintenance, which is generated when an AJC family terminates in mid-month. AJC pays the
family only for the time they put in at AJC, but DVR pays maintenance
on a whole family/month basis.

AJC also receives funds from various sources, which are treated
by its accounting system as "reductions in expenditures" rather than
income items. These funds are of interest to DOL since they are used
to reduce the draws on the DOL grant account. These items and the
amounts for the indicated fiscal years are as follows:

	Fiscal Year 1971	Fiscal Year 1972	Fiscal Year 1973	First Half of Fiscal Year 1974
	(in thousands of dollars)			
Rental of houses to AJC families	4.9	58.2	55.5	24.7
School lunches	2.7	10.0	4.5	0.9
Lunches sold to employees	1.0	2.4	0.6	.0
DVR maintenance	14.8	57.8	71.1	48.8
DVR driving	2.4	10.0	0.6	.0
Totals	25.8	138.4	132.3	74.4

The first item above is concerned with how the AJC system
treats the expenses of renting houses for AJC families. These houses
have been rented from private parties in Casa Grande and from the Pinal
County Housing Authority. AJC pays rents out of its DOL grant account.
AJC also collects rent for the houses from the families who occupy these
houses. The total rent that AJC collects is put back into the DOL grant

account. This procedure really amounts to a rent subsidy for AJC families, since AJC is actually subletting the houses to its families at a loss.

With regard to the second and third items above, AJC's cafeteria sold lunches to employees and derived some income from this source. The state of Arizona, under its school lunch program, reimburses AJC for the expenses incurred in feeding preschool children at lunchtime. The money obtained from these sources is also used to reduce the draw against the DOL grant account.

DVR pays its clients an amount for "maintenance" during their training periods. Since each AJC family is a DVR client, AJC is able to offset the family's stipend by the DVR maintenance payment. DVR also pays its clients an amount for transportation from their homes to their training sites. AJC utilizes this source of income to offset its rented vehicle expense. Since stipends and rented vehicle expenses are both paid for out of the DOL grant account, the fourth and fifth items in the table above both contribute to reducing the draw against it.

The purpose of this lengthy description of AJC's finances has been to show how complicated the establishment of a comprehensive family rehabilitation program can be in a society whose social welfare system is an uncoordinated, messy group of piecemeal programs. Obviously, keeping track of all the various funding sources with their different calendars for the grant application process, made "grants-manship" a full-time job at AJC. The periodic expiration of different grants at various times also plunged AJC into a semipermanent state of crisis – some source of money was always ending, threatening to bring down the entire program with it.

MOBILIZATION OF FINANCIAL RESOURCES

Throughout its history, one of the main thrusts of OEO has been the mobilization of resources for the reduction of poverty. Some resources to help poor people existed before OEO's birth and continue to exist. However, in many cases the poor are unable to use these resources for one reason or another. For example, red tape required to utilize existing services, such as Farmer's Home Administration housing loans or the U.S. Department of Agriculture's food programs, made these programs largely unavailable to the poor people that the programs were supposed to help. OEO provided programs at compara-tively low costs which were designed to help the poor utilize these existing programs.

Development of Non-OEO Grants. In the case of AJC, the OEO grant mobilized a large amount of existing resources which were in the form of tied-up grants. At the time that OEO made its grant, AJC already had approximately $1,466,400 in non-OEO grants. These grant funds were, however, unavailable for use because of "matching money" constraints. The Ford Foundation grant, which was to supply matching funds for grants from HUD (for facilities and initial staffing), could not yet be utilized because of the Ford Foundation's requirement that AJC receive $5.5 million in federal grants over a three-year period. The OEO grant made the total existing federal grant money for AJC's first year of operation enough, on a yearly basis, to release the Ford Foundation funds. Thus, the immediate return on OEO's investment in AJC was 360 percent, in that OEO's granting AJC $550,000 mobilized over $2 million to carry out OEO's mission to fight poverty.

Estimated Values of Additional Resources Mobilized

AJC's existence has resulted in the mobilization of a variety of other resources, both public and private to help target population. Included in these resources are:

1. Time spent by AJC Board of Directors. AJC's 18-man Board donates an average of four man-hours a month to AJC business. Assuming that Board members' time is worth $10 an hour* (the Board is made up of business and professional leaders) this amounts on the average to $720 worth of services each month.

2. Time spent by Industrial Advisory Council (IAC) members. When operable, the 18-man Industrial Advisory Council will meet for approximately two hours each month. Making the same assumptions as above, this resource will eventually amount to $360 each month.

3. Time spent by Community Advisory Council (CAC) members. This group is composed mainly of nonprofessionals; hence their time is assumed to be worth $5 an hour, which amounts to a total resource of $180 each month.

4. Materials and services from the Arizona Division of Vocational Rehabilitation. DVR provides each year, on the average, resources to each AJC family:

Resource	Value
Medical exams	$ 45
Eyeglasses	40
Dentures	150

---

*These and other estimates of the values of man-hours were obtained using OEO Instruction 6802-1, "Valuation of Volunteered Personal Services for Purposes of Computing the Non-Federal Share."

Resource	Value
Testing and vocational evaluation services	$ 120
Tuition	600
Supplies	50
Maintenance and transportation	300
Total	$1,305

At AJC's eventual operating level of 120 families, this re-source will amount to $13,050 each month. At the average level of 16 families which AJC operated at during fiscal year 1971, DVR-supplied resources amounted to $1,740 each month.

5. Volunteer services. AJC received the following volunteer services during fiscal year 1971: A. Neighborhood Youth Corps—833 man-hours/month $1.60/man-hour, or $1,333/month. B. Vista—1,204 man-hours/month $5/man/hour or $6,020/month. C. Legal Aid—$20 man-hours/month $20/man-hour or $400/month. D. Recruiting—a CAP delegate agency, "Grassroots," contributes about 8 man-hours/month recruiting families for AJC $5/man-hour, or $40/month. AJC's volunteer services are worth a total amount of $7,793 each month.

6. Federal government excess property. AJC is currently utilizing federal excess property valued at $214,567. Assuming a purchase price to monthly lease cost ratio of 40:1, this resource amounts to $5,364 a month.

7. Arizona Department of Health (ASDH). In the second half of AJC's fiscal year 1971, ASDH granted $8,616 to AJC to initiate a health program. Averaged out over the year, this resource has a value of $718 a month.

8. Miscellaneous. Other resources mobilized by AJC in be-half of its client-families include: (A) Parent-Child Center (PCC)—a Casa Grande church donated its recreational hall to AJC for use as a PCC during the summer of 1970, until AJC was able to get its own PCC into operation; estimated value, $300. (B) Commodity Distribution—AJC assists its client-families to take advantage of Pinal County's Commodity Distribution program, through assisting in the paperwork necessary for qualification and in providing the means to transport the commodities from the warehouse to the families' homes; estimated value, $20 each family-month. (C) Pinal County Health Department, to the extent that it precipitated a crisis at the Casa Grande Health Center (see the discussion above). (D) Contributions— a Phoenix bank contributed $250 to AJC. Based on the estimated values of the above resources and an average family-month level of 16 during fiscal year 1971, the total value of miscellaneous resources amounted to $450 a month.

EXPENDITURES

Table 5.3 show the history of monthly operating costs and amounts of OEO and DOL funds utilized by AJC through November 1973; these amounts are presented in columns 1 and 2, respectively. The average number of families enrolled at AJC for each month is also shown.

From an evaluation standpoint, Table 5.3 reveals some interesting aspects of AJC's operations over the years. Column 4 shows how the fraction of AJC's operating costs borne by the OEO/DOL grants has fluctuated monthly around its overall average of 53 percent. This illustrates how AJC's original goal of an enrollment of 125 residential families was attempted but given up when it became clear that the facilities and staff were not able to adequately handle that many families. Column 5 indicates that AJC's staff has continued to grow steadily during the program's existence. Columns 6, 7, and 8 all show sharp increases during recent times. The increases in columns 6 and 8, the monthly operating costs each residential family-month and the number of staff-months for each family-month, are partly explainable by AJC's expansion in services (medical, services to welfare recipients, and so on) to nonresidential rural poor families. Staff and budget increases are necessary to provide these extracurricular services. And since the number of residential families remains fairly constant, the ratios in columns 6 and 8 increase dramatically. Increases in the ratios in column 7 are attributable to increasing training costs for the average AJC residential family, which is, in turn, related to the high rate of inflation in recent months.

Figure 5, has been prepared to graphically illustrate some of the statistics contained in Table 5.3. It is evident that the staff size has continued to climb, on the average, even though the number of families "peaked out" at the end of AJC's second year. While the number of families seems to be levelling off at about 70, there is no indication that staff size is levelling off. Also, as was mentioned above, the operating cost each family-month and the number of staff members for each family after remaining fairly stable during most of the second year of operation have recently been moving up.

Table 5.4 has been prepared in order to examine operating costs from a slightly different viewpoint. Since the AJC Medical department now operates almost as an independent program with independent funding, and because of the nature of the medical program, (serving nonresident as well as resident families) it is useful to look at AJC operating costs excluding those attributable to the Medical department. Thus, Table 5.4 presents recalculations of some of the same statistics in Table 5.3, with the Medical department costs excluded.

Figure 6 presents the data from Table 5.4 in graphic form. This figure illustrates the increasing trend in operating costs, excluding

TABLE 5.3

Operating Costs, OEO/DOL Expenditures, Personnel Levels, and Related Statistics
(All monetary dimensions are in thousands of dollars)

	(1) Operating Costs Excluding Construction and Trailers	(2) Amounts Drawn From OEO/DOL Funds	(3) Fraction of Operating Cost Paid For With OEO/DOL Funds (2)/(1)	(4) Average Number of Residential Families During Month	(5) Average Staff Size During Month	(6) Cost Each Family-Month (1)/(4)	(7) OEO/DOL "Draw" Each Family-Month (2)/(4)	(8) Staff Members for Each Residential Family (5)/(4)
June 1970	36.8	30.4	.83	5	20	7.36	6.08	4.00
July	29.4	18.7	.64	8	22	3.68	2.34	2.75
August	34.2	23.7	.69	10	23	3.42	2.37	2.30
September	37.0	24.9	.67	10	25	3.70	2.49	2.50
October	38.5	26.4	.69	10	24	3.85	2.64	2.40
November	31.6	20.0	.63	10	25	3.16	2.00	2.50
December	30.9	19.1	.62	10	27	3.09	1.91	2.70
January 1971	31.5	35.7[a]	.70[e]	10	28	3.15[e]	2.22[e]	2.80
February	58.9	22.0	.37	15	49	3.93	1.47	3.27
March	70.5[a]	50.4[b]	.59[e]	20	49	2.43[e]	1.42[e]	2.45
April	53.5	33.2	.62	25	49	2.14	1.33	1.96
May	59.2	31.7	.54	30	50	1.97	1.06	1.67
June	64.7	25.3	.39	38	54	1.70[f]	.67[e]	1.42
July	151.0[c]	123.4[c]	.72[e]	54	60	1.81	1.30	1.11
August[d]	70.1	42.6	.61	70	61	1.00	.61	.87
September	81.2	44.2	.54	74	66	1.10	.60	.89
October	91.9	57.3	.62	81	70	1.13	.71	.86
November	91.8	49.6	.54	87	72	1.06	.57	.83
December	96.1	58.0	.60	86	72	1.12	.67	.84
January 1972	81.8	42.8	.52	92	69	.89	.47	.75
February	117.1	67.7	.58	99	68	1.18	.68	.69
March	97.6	57.2	.59	99	68	.99	.58	.69
April	140.7	68.7	.49	104	72	1.35	.66	.69
May	108.6	41.7	.38	106	73	1.02	.39	.69
June	128.0	65.7	.51	107	72	1.20	.61	.67
July	91.9	51.6	.56	98	72	.94	.53	.73
August	113.6	57.5	.51	92	78	1.23	.63	.85
September	102.0	48.0	.47	88	77	1.16	.55	.88
October	112.3	57.5	.51	84	79	1.34	.68	.94
November	112.5	54.0	.48	86	79	1.31	.63	.92
December	113.7	54.2	.48	87	84	1.32	.62	.97
January 1973	108.2	36.5	.34	79	86	1.37	.46	1.09
February	88.6	31.0	.35	75	89	1.16	.41	1.19
March	139.5	61.1[f]	.44	72	92	1.78	.23	1.39
April	124.8	50.2	.40	73	91	1.71	.69	1.25
May	115.7	71.9	.62	72	95	1.61	1.00	1.32
June	145.4	32.9	.23	73	89	1.99	.45	1.22
July	111.7[g]	61.8	.55	73	100	1.53	.85	1.37
August	129.3[g]	69.8	.54	72	107	1.80	.97	1.49
September	157.5[g]	70.6	.45	65	105	2.42	1.09	1.62
October	125.6[g]	64.3	.51	65	104	1.93	.99	1.60
November	144.4[g]	81.3	.56	70	110	2.06	1.16	1.57
42-Month Average	92.1	48.4	.53	69.4	68	1.33	.70	.98

[a]Includes $13,500 drawn from OEO account to reimburse Ford Foundation General Fund for money spent earlier for air conditioning the trailers.

[b]Includes $22,000 for transportation of federally-owned surplus equipment.

[c]Includes $53,000 for special program equipment (home furnishings for AJC families).

[d]Second OEO grant period begins.

[e]The figures mentioned in the above footnotes have been subtracted from operating costs and/or the OEO account draw prior to calculting this quantity.

[f]OEO/DOL Migrant funding begins.

[g]Estimated by adding 30.0 per month for Medical Dept. to AJC nonmedical operating costs.

142

FIGURE 5

Staff Size, Number of Families, and Related Statistics
June 1970-November 1973

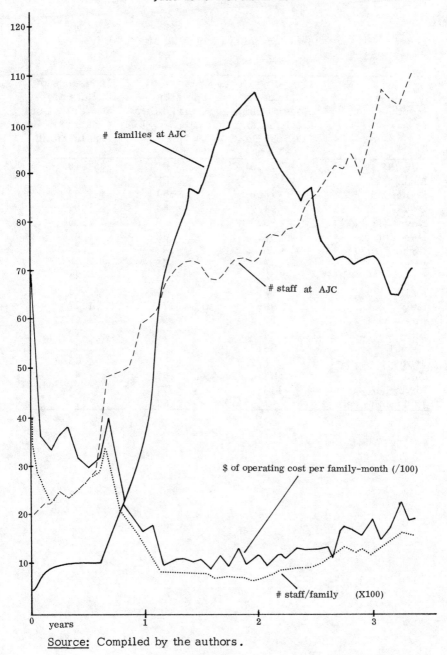

Source: Compiled by the authors.

143

TABLE 5.4

Operating Costs (Excluding Medical)

Month	Operating Costs Excluding Construction, Trailers, and Medical Dept. Costs	Fraction of Operating Cost Paid for with OEO/DOL Funds	Thousands of Dollars of Operating Cost Each Family–Month
July 1972	76.0	.68	.78
August	87.1	.66	.95
September	78.8	.61	.90
October	91.7	.63	1.09
November	90.6	.60	1.05
December	87.7	.62	1.01
January 1973	75.3	.48	.95
February	68.9	.45	.92
March	94.3	.65	1.31
April	82.4	.61	1.13
May	98.7	.73	1.37
June	122.1	.27	1.67
July	86.2	.72	1.18
August	99.3	.70	1.38
September	108.9	.65	1.68
October	95.6	.67	1.47
November	114.4	.71	1.63
17-Month Average	91.6	.61	1.18

FIGURE 6

Operating Costs and Number of Residential Families
July 1972-November 1973

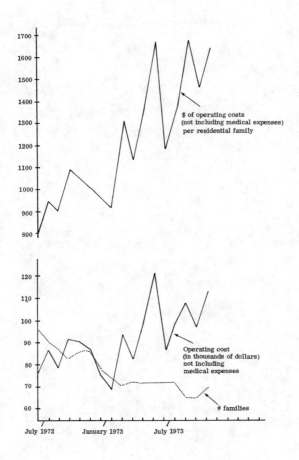

Source: Compiled by the authors.

TABLE 5.5

Departmental Expenses by Type for Fiscal Year 1973
(thousands of dollars)

Expenses	Administration	Adm-Family Services	Counseling	Job Development and Employment	Recruiting	Vocational Evaluation	Total Family Serv.	Special Serv. Adm	Special Services	Home Living Services	Total Spec. Serv.
Salaries, wages, payroll taxes, and benefits	68.9	22.8	50.0	16.5	4.4	10.4	104.1	4.9	29.5	33.0	67.4
Consultants	.5	-	-	-	-	-	-	-	-	-	.3
Travel expenses	16.9	.1	.6	.1	-	-	.8	-	.3	-	.3
Rent, Improvements, maintenance, and utilities	1.9	-	-	-	-	2.2	2.2	-	-	.1	.1
Materials and supplies (excludes supplies for clients)	3.0	.1	.3	.1	.1	.3	.9	-	2.9	4.7	7.6
Beneficiary costs: Stipends, medical service, housing, supplies, cultural enrichment	-	-	-	.1	-	1.1	1.2	-	.2	6.2	6.4
Business expenses (employee recruiting, repairs, telephone, postage, insurance)	45.3	.2	.2	.3	-	27.9	28.6	-	1.0	-	1.0
Rent-furniture and furnishings, vehicles, office and program equipment	26.1	-	-	-	-	-	-	-	.1	-	.1
Land and buildings	14.9	-	-	-	-	-	-	-	-	-	-
Program equipment	.6	-	-	-	-	-	-	-	-	.1	.1
Vehicles	-	-	-	-	-	-	-	-	-	-	-
Trailers	-	-	-	-	-	-	-	-	-	-	-
Totals	178.1	23.2	51.1	17.1	4.5	41.9	137.8	4.9	34.0	44.1	83.0

Expenses	Instruction Adm.	Instruction	Total Instruction	Bus. Office-Adm.	Fiscal Maint.	Housing and Maint.	Property Control	Stipends	Total Bus. Office (AJC)	Medical	Medical	Child Development	Total Medical	Grand Totals
Salaries, wages, payroll taxes, and benefits	20.6	27.1	47.7	24.2	23.5	79.8	16.5	-	144.0	-	144.2	94.7	238.9	671.0
Consultants	-	-	-	1.7	5.4	-	-	-	7.1	-	.5	-	.5	8.1
Travel expenses	-	.2	.2	-	-	.2	-	-	.2	-	11.2	.5	11.7	30.1
Rent, improvements, maintenance, and utilities	-	-	-	14.2	-	32.6	-	-	46.8	-	6.2	-	6.2	57.2
Materials and supplies (excludes supplies for clients)	.4	2.8	3.2	3.7	.4	18.0	3.3	-	25.4	-	10.8	6.4	17.2	57.3
Beneficiary costs: Stipends, medical service, housing, supplies, cultural enrichment	-	2.2	2.2	25.5	.4	4.0	5.0	170.6	205.5	18.8	94.5[a]	8.9	122.2	337.5
Business expenses (employee recruiting, repairs, telephone, postage, insurance)	.3	24.6	24.9	(12.1)	.4	17.2	4.6	-	10.1	-	35.3	2.1	37.4	147.3
Rent-furniture and furnishings, vehicles, office and program equipment	-	.2	.2	12.0	-	.3	.1	-	12.4	-	1.7	-	1.7	40.5
Land and buildings	-	-	-	-	-	-	-	-	-	-	-	-	-	14.9
Program equipment	-	.1	.1	-	-	2.8	1.0	-	3.8	-	1.6	.1	1.7	6.3
Vehicles	-	-	-	-	-	-	-	-	-	-	4.2	-	4.2	4.2
Trailers	-	-	-	-	-	-	-	-	-	-	8.7	-	8.7	8.7
Totals	21.3	57.2	78.5	69.2	30.1	154.9	30.5	170.6	455.3	18.8	318.9	112.7	450.4	1383.1

[a]Non-AJC and AJC "day student" families

all medical expenses, for the period from July 1972 to November 1973. This tendency to increase occurred despite the fact that there was a general decreasing trend in the number of residential families over this period. The operating cost, less medical, for each residential family consequently has increased dramatically over this period of time.

Table 5.5 provides breakdowns of individual departments' expenditures in fiscal year 1973. The increased ratio of staff to enrolled families and the accompanying increase in cost for each family was in large part due to AJC's complex financial system and to the resulting state of constant fiscal crisis. Early in 1973 the Nixon administration mounted a determined effort to destroy OEO, leading to considerable confusion and doubts about the future of OEO projects. At the same time, AJC was running out of OEO money and was unable to get a firm commitment from OEO for future funds. Not wishing to make commitments to client-families it might not have been able to keep, AJC drastically reduced the intake of new families into the program during this period. However, a staff had been built up to operate a program with more families than were enrolled; consequently, the cost for each family began to rise. Because of the OEO financial crisis AJC sought alternative sources of funds to save the program. The only alternative found was the Arizona state grant to provide services to nonresidential welfare clients. Although this money stabilized AJC's financial problem by having something the facilities and staff could be used for, it shifted staff away from the residential family program, thereby increasing the number of staff for each residential family.

6

TRAINING COSTS

Tables 5.3 and 5.4 provide data for calculating the average training cost for each residential family. Since its inception, AJC has accomplished 2856 family-months of training with operating costs, including medical costs, of $3.8682 million, an average of $1354 for each family-month of training, or $16,253 for each family-year of training. Based on an average family size of 5.2, this amounts to an annual training cost for each individual of $3126. During fiscal year 1973 and all the months following for which cost data were available up to the time of writing, AJC has provided 1324 family-months of training for an operating cost, including medical services of $2.0367 million. Thus, for a recent 17-month period, the average cost of a family-month of training has been $1538, or $18,460 for each family-year.

Utilizing Table 5.4 exactly as Table 5.3 was used above, the operating costs, excluding medical costs, were $1.5572 million over the past 17 months, for an average of $1176 for each family-month or $14,114 for each family-year. On an individual basis (again using the average family size of 5.2), annual training costs, excluding medical costs, amount to $2714.

Since roughly half the medical costs are spent on AJC families, half of the difference between the average cost including medical and the average cost not including medical added to the latter yields the average rehabilitation cost attributable to AJC families. This operation for the 17 months shown in Table 5.4 yields a figure of $1,357 for each family-month, or $16,284 for each family year.

Because of the effect of the dropouts, AJC actually exposes a larger number of families to its rehabilitation program than the number of graduates would indicate. The average length of time a dropout spends at AJC is 4.3 months. Since the dropout rate is approximately 50

149

percent, the average length of time at AJC for all families, graduates
and dropouts, is

.5 x 4.3 months + .5 x 12 months or 8.15 months

Hence, the average cost of exposing a family to the AJC rehabilitation
program is

8.15 x $1,357, or 11,060

Still another method (suggested by Frank Harris, consultant to
the Ford Foundation) of allocating training costs is to first calculate
the total cost of exposing a dropout family to the program which is

$1357 x 4.3 months, or $5835

Then, since the average time in the program for dropout families is 4.3
months, as opposed to 12 months for graduates, the processing rate for
dropout families is 2.8 times that of graduating families. Hence in
order to sustain the 1973 graduation rate of 44 families a year, 2.8 x
44, or 124 dropout families must be processed in that year. This assumes
that any entering group of families is composed half of eventual dropouts
and half of eventual graduates. The annual costs for processing these
dropouts therefore amounts to 124 x $5835, or $723,540. Assuming
annual operating costs, including one-half of the medical costs, of
$1.2684 million, there is then $544,860 left for processing the graduating families, or a cost of $12,383 for each graduating family.

The Department of Labor often determines the cost of job placements for a year in evaluating training programs. If we take 1973, in
which AJC placed 59 individuals in jobs, utilizing information in Table
5.4, we find that AJC's total cost for each job placement was, using
the annual operating cost attributed to AJC families, $1,268,400 di-
vided by 59, or $21,498 for each job placement.

As is illustrated by the above paragraphs, statistics on AJC
training costs vary widely according to definition, and the period of time
over which they are calculated.

RETURN-ON-INVESTMENT

This subsection considers one aspect of society's economic
return from AJC, the amount of money returned to the government in the
form of new taxes generated by the graduates of AJC who have become
more affluent than they were before.

In calculating the financial return (see Becker 1964 for a theoretical discussion of the ideas upon which this section is based) to the

government, it is assumed that the total economic benefit generated
by AJC includes the following components:

- state and federal income taxes generated by AJC graduate-
  families
- additional state and federal income taxes generated as a
  result of the "economic multiplier" effect
- the additional state sales tax generated through increasing
  the salary levels of AJC graduate families
- the savings in public assistance costs resulting from the
  rehabilitation of AJC graduate families

Inclusion of the returns from state taxes assumes that the federal
government's economic objectives relative to sponsoring AJC include
increasing the financial benefits to the state government also.
    The calculation of the estimated total economic benefits from
AJC, utilizing the four factors listed above, will err on the conserv-
ative side. The monetary returns generated from such items as taxes
and property taxes have not been included, due to the excessive effort
required to obtain accurate statistics on them.
    The economic gains that will eventually be realized from the
children of AJC families have only been included for one generation.
If AJC is successful in breaking the "cycle of poverty," the eventual
economic impact, from the rehabilitation of AJC children, their children, their children's children, and so on, will be enormous. However,
the average age of the sample families' children is 5.9 years, so that
the initial contribution, on the average, from the children's economic
rehabilitation will occur approximately 15 years after the family graduates from AJC. The return-on-investment calculation presented later
in this section projects the next 40 years, so the economic returns
from the grandchildren of AJC families have no effect on it.
    Each of the four components of the economic benefits from AJC
listed above is discussed in more detail in the subsections immediately
following.

State and Federal Income Taxes Generated by AJC Graduate-Families.
It is assumed that an average AJC family paid no income taxes prior
to admission to AJC. The data on entering AJC families gives an average
family size of 5.23 and an average annual family income of $2,616.
The federal income tax tables indicate that a family of five pays no tax
until its income reaches $4,250.
    The projected income tax for AJC graduate-families during their
first year after graduation can be calculated according to standard
methods outlined for U.S. Form 1040. Average salaries for AJC graduate families four months after graduation are $6,241 a year. Applying
the income tax calculations, we have:

gross income	$6,241
less: 13 percent standard deduction	− 811
less: exemptions (5.23 average AJC family size multiplied by $750/ exemption)	−3,923
taxable income	$1,507
federal income tax	216

In subsequent years, family income of AJC graduates will increase through salary increases. Consequently, the income tax component of this monetary benefit will increase. Assuming an average annual increase of r percent, due solely to productivity (that is, not to inflation), the annual salary for the average AJC graduate family will be

$$S = \$6241 \times (1+r/100)^{n-1} \tag{1}$$

during the nth year after graduation. The formula for the taxable income during the nth year, assuming the 13 percent standard deduction is taken, is therefore

$$I = .87 \times \$6241 \times (1+r/100)^{n-1} - \$3923 \tag{2}$$

The federal income tax is, then,

$$T = \begin{cases} \$140 + .15 \times (I-\$1000) & \text{for } \$1000 < I \leq \$2000 \\ \$290 + .16 \times (I-\$2000) & \text{for } \$2000 < I \leq \$3000 \\ \$450 + .17 \times (I-\$3000) & \text{for } \$3000 < I \leq \$4000 \\ \$620 + .19 \times (I-\$4000) & \text{for } \$4000 < I \leq \$8000 \\ \$1380 + .22 \times (I-\$8000) & \text{for } \$8000 < I \leq \$12,000 \\ \$2260 + .25 \times (I-\$12,000) & \text{for } \$12,000 < I \leq \$16,000 \end{cases} \tag{3}$$

These formulas were from the tax table. Taxable income is limited to $16,000 in the calculation.

In addition to the federal income tax, AJC families will begin paying state income taxes. Arizona state income tax amounts to approximately 10 percent of the Federal tax. It is assumed, therefore, that the total state and federal income taxes paid by AJC graduates in the first year after graduation will be $216 + $22, or $238. In general, if the federal income tax during the nth year after graduation is denoted by T_n, the state income tax will be assumed to be $T_n/10$.

State and Federal Taxes Generated as a Result of the Economic Multiplier Effect. The idea behind the economic multiplier effect is that any "new money" which is added to an economic domain accounts for an expansion of that economic domain which is over and above that caused solely by the addition of the money itself. The Arizona Department

of Economic Planning and Development recently developed some multi-
pliers for Casa Grande; the particular statistic of interest here is that
each additional dollar resulting from an AJC graduate's increased productivity generates 90¢ of additional economic activity (Storm 1972)
which includes such factors as service personnel salaries and retail
sales. It is assumed here that eventually some individual or corporate
entity pays income tax on that 90¢. The average income for residents
of Pinal County is $8700, and the average family size is 3.2. The
income tax paid by the average Casa Grande citizen is then calculated
as follows:

gross income	$8,700
less: 13 percent standard deduction	-1,131
less: exemptions (3.5 multiplied by $750)	-2,625
taxable income	$4,944
federal income tax	800
state income tax	80

The federal and state income tax is 880/8700, or .101 of the average
individual gross income.

The following formula is used to calculate the additional state
and federal income taxes generated from the multiplier effect applied
to an individual family's salary:

$$M = .101 \times .9 \times (S - 1.1T - X - \$2616) \qquad (4)$$

The term within parenthesis is the average annual projected salary
from equation (1) less the state and federal income taxes, the sales
tax X calculated from equation (5) (below), and the salary prior to
entering AJC. The latter is subtracted from the present salary to account
for the fact that $2616 of that total amount was present before the fam-
ily was trained at AJC. Formula (4) multiplies this amount by the 90¢
of additional economic activity and by the fraction of this activity
which goes into income taxes (.101).

Additional State Sales Tax Generated. As was mentioned earlier, an
average AJC family's income before entering AJC is $2,616 and the family
size was 5.3. The optional state sales tax tables in the federal income
tax instruction booklet estimate that such a family paid $65 per year
in Arizona state sales tax. The first year after graduation, the same
family is expected to gross $6,241 on the average. The sales tax tables
estimate that this family will then pay $121 a year in sales tax, for a
net increase of $56 a year over that paid before entering AJC. The
following formula is an estimate of the additional Arizona state sales
tax, according to the sales tax tables, paid by the average AJC-trained
family after graduation:

$$X = 56 + 10.5 \text{ X } (S-6000) / 1,000 \qquad\qquad (5)$$

where S is the salary determined from (1).

Savings in Public Assistance Costs. The date on entering families
reveals that, on the average, the public assistance cost for AJC families
prior to entrance is \$515 a year. After graduation, of course, public
assistance for the family will not be necessary, so that society will
be saved this expense as a result of AJC's existence.

Total Monetary Benefits from AJC. The total monetary benefit to all
levels of government from taxes paid by an employed average AJC
graduate-family during the nth year after graduation is

$$B_n = 1.1T_n + X_n + M_n + \$515 \qquad\qquad (6)$$

Subscripts are used to denote time dependence. The first term on the
right-hand side of (6) is the state and federal income tax, with T_n
being calculated from (3). The second term is the sales tax calculated
from (5). The third term is the amount due to the multiplier effect,
from equation (4). The last term accounts for the annual saving in
public assistance cost.

The quantity B_n is the amount of benefits generated by a single
family during its nth year after graduation. Thus, an individual family
will generate B_1 in benefits for the first year after it completes training
at AJC, B_2 in benefits will be generated the second year, B_3 the third,
and so on. In what follows, the term "benefit-generating family-year"
(or sometimes simply "family-year") is used to connote a year that an
average AJC graduate family is generating income and spending money
from which government derives tax revenues.

In the latter half of fiscal year 1972, AJC began to "graduate"
families into the world of work. Because of the fiscal year 1972 graduation schedule (12 in February 1972, with 20 more between March 1
and June 30, 1972), 32 families generated benefits of B_1 from 1972 to
1973. During fiscal year 1973, 44 families were graduated, so from
1973 to 1974, 44 family-years will generate benefits of B_1, and 32
family-years will generate benefits of B_2. Table 6.1 has been prepared to show the number of families which generate the different levels
of benefits during fiscal years 1973 and beyond. Table 6.1 is continued
only through fiscal year 1978, since the overall trend is discernible
from the picture in the initial years.

The formulas for calculating the total returns from taxes for each
year can be written down directly by referring to Table 6.1:

$$
\begin{aligned}
&1973: \ G_1 = 32 \, B_1 \qquad\qquad\qquad\qquad\qquad\qquad (7)\\
&1974: \ G_2 = 44 \, B_1 + 32 \, B_2 \\
&1975: \ G_3 = 44 \, B_1 + 44 \, B_2 + 32 \, B_3
\end{aligned}
$$

1976: $G_4 = 44 (B_1 + B_2 + B_3) + 32 B_4$
1977: $G_5 = 44 (B_1 + B_2 + B_3 + B_4) + 32 B_5$

and so on, where G_n denotes the total gains from all benefits attributable to AJC families in year n.

TABLE 6.1

Schedule of Benefit-Generating Family-Years

Fiscal Year	Number of Families Each Generating Annual Benefits Equal to B_n					
	B_1	B_2	B_3	B_4	B_5	B_6
1973	32	–	–	–	–	–
1974	44	32	–	–	–	–
1975	44	44	32	–	–	–
1976	44	44	44	32	–	–
1977	44	44	44	44	32	–
1978	44	44	44	44	44	32

Effects of the gains from AJC children are represented by adding 3.3 (the average number of children in an AJC family) multiplied by G_1 to G_{17}, 3.3 multiplied by G_2 to G_{18}, and so forth. Thus, it is assumed that each child will generate, sixteen years hence, the same benefits as his parents did. The sixteen-year time period was arrived at by subtracting the (truncated) average age of AJC children, 5.9 years, from 21. Truncation was chosen over rounding because of the younger age of current AJC families. The present value* of all gains over the next n years is

$$H_N = \sum_{n=1}^{N} G_n / (1+i)^n \qquad (8)$$

---

*The "present value" of a monetary return R which is collectable n years hence is $R/(1+i)^n$, where i is the average interest rate in effect over the period of time between now and the time of collection. The present value can also be thought of as the amount which must be invested now, at the interest rate i which is compounded annually, in order to obtain n years hence an amount R. The use of the present value concept allows us to properly weight costs and benefits according to when they are incurred.

where i is the average interest rate over the N-year period and G_n is determined from equations (7).

AJC Operating Costs. The following schedule presents past and projected annual costs for AJC, in thousands of dollars:

Fiscal Year	Federal Cost	Nonfederal Cost
1969	59.7	23.5
1970	165.4	80.0
1971	813.5	320.9
1972	943.0	340.0
1973 and beyond	1100.0	300.0

The fiscal year 1973 operating cost was used for the annual operating costs projected beyond 1973, since AJC seems to have achieved its steady-state operating level.

The present value of all federal costs out to N years beyond fiscal year 1973 is, then:

$$C_N = 1981.6 + \sum_{n=1}^{N} 1100/(1+i)^n \qquad (9)$$

Calculation of the Return-on-Investment. The ratio

$$R_N = H_N / C_N \qquad (10)$$

is the return on the government's investment in AJC, where 11_N and C_N are "present values" of the total gains over the next N years and the costs over the next N years, respectively.

Values of R_N were calculated out to 40 years for several different combinations of values of r, the average rate of salary increases for AJC families, and i, the average interest rate. Table 6.2 summarizes the results of this calculation. Table 6.2 has four different subtables. Values for two different values of r are presented for each of two different values of i.

The most optimistic case in Table 6.2 is for i = 0 and r = .05, in which case AJC would break even sometime between the year 1995 and 2000. The most pessimistic case, i = .1 and r = 0, shows AJC yielding, by 2010, only 46¢ on each federal dollar invested. A likely case, i = .1 and r = .05, predicts a 2010 return of 77¢ on each federal dollar invested in AJC. The case where i = 0 and r = 0 gives the results for the case where interest rates and rates of salary increase are ignored.

As we indicated earlier, the calculation errs on the side of reducing the federal return-on-investment, since we have not included many of the "hidden" taxes paid by the middle class.

TABLE 6.2

Federal Return-on-Investment (ROI) in AJC
(costs and gains are in thousands of dollars)

Year	Costs*	r = 0		r = .05	
		Gains	ROI	Gains	ROI
i = 0					
1975	5281.6	213.0	.04	219.2	.04
1980	10781.6	1403.3	.13	1600.4	.15
1985	16281.6	3742.2	.23	4791.3	.29
1990	21781.6	7229.6	.33	10455.8	.48
1995	27281.6	14070.7	.52	21887.6	.80
2000	32781.6	25735.7	.79	42966.6	1.31
2005	38281.6	42224.7	1.10	76905.2	2.01
2010	43781.6	63537.5	1.45	126926.3	2.90
i = .1					
1975	4817.1	174.3	.04	179.1	.04
1980	7950.0	827.5	.10	932.6	.12
1985	9895.3	1639.3	.17	2033.0	.21
1990	11103.2	2395.6	.22	3253.1	.29
1995	11853.1	3303.5	.28	4769.5	.40
2000	12318.8	4275.6	.35	6518.3	.53
2005	12608.0	5132.9	.41	8273.9	.66
2010	12787.5	5822.6	.46	9884.6	.77

*actual costs since the interest rate i is zero
Note: i = interest rate, r = average rate of salary increase.

COMPARISON OF AJC
WITH OTHER MANPOWER TRAINING PROGRAMS

The purpose of this subsection is to present some conclusions
about how AJC compares with other training programs funded by the
Manpower Administration. To this end benefit/cost ratios were calculated from data presented in RMC (1969) and ORC (1971). The "benefits"
part of this ratio is that defined in RMC:

Benefits = (salary gain) x (employment rate)

The salary gain is simply the post-training salary, measured several
months after completion of training, less the pretraining salary, the
average pay rate for the year immediately prior to the training program.

The employment rate is the fraction of trainees placed at the end of the training period who are still working when the follow-up measurement is made.

RMC develops benefit/cost ratios for Neighborhood Youth Corps (NYC) and Job Corps trainees on a nationwide basis. Data from two surveys are utilized, a follow-up survey of 2000 NYC trainees conducted nine months after completion of training, and a survey of 900 Job Corp trainees conducted at 6 and 18 months after completion of training.

ORC presents a wealth of data on Manpower-Administration-financed programs gathered from a variety of sources. The Concentrated Employment Program (CEP) contains many of the same program components as AJC, such as child care, stipends, medical services, job development, and placement, and hence was selected for inclusion on that basis. Programs in Denver and in the San Francisco Bay Area were selected because of their relative proximity to the geographic area served by AJC. The Richmond, California CEP was utilized because placement and follow-up data for the Oakland CEP were not included in ORC.

The Work Incentive Program (WIN), as described in ORC, also appears to include components similar to AJC's, although child care and medical assistance, not included in WIN, are arranged through other agencies by the WIN counselor or caseworker. Again, the Denver and Bay Area WIN programs were selected for inclusion. Of particular interest is the fact that the distribution of WIN-Denver participants' ethnic backgrounds is similar to that of AJC.

Data on the various programs considered are presented in Table 6.3.

AJC's follow-up data were utilized to develop a graduate-family average salary of $6527. The pre-AJC average of $2616 for graduates (that is, nondropouts) obtained from the study sample was utilized to estimate pre-AJC annual salaries for this group, since no data are available. Evidence for the reasonableness of this estimate is found in Table 3.5, which indicates that the average pre-AJC hourly wage remained constant over a sixteen month time period. It is assumed that the percentage of time employed before coming to AJC does not increase with time either. Of the 44 families who graduated in 1973, there were three in which neither adult member was employed when contacted by the AJC follow-up coordinator. The average length of time between exit and the follow-up contacts for this group was six months.

To calculate the cost for each trained family of AJC's 1973 graduates, operating costs for the 24-month period covering the time when these graduates were at AJC must be considered. The following steps were used to calculate the cost for each trained family:

TABLE 6.3

Benefit/Cost Ratio Comparisons for Manpower Programs

	(1) Pre- to Post-Training Annual Salary Increase (dollars)	(2) Percent Employed	(3) Cost for Each Trainee-Month[a]	(4) Average Length of Time in Program (month)	(5) Cost for Each Trainee-Month[a]	B/C Ratio A (1) x (2)/(3)	B/C Ratio B (1) x (2)/5
AJC families (1973 graduates)	$3911	93	$32,232	12	$2686	.113	1.35
AJC families (study sample graduates)	3598	67	22,584	12	1882	.107	1.28
Job Corps (women)	135	50	3,840	5.2	738	.018	.09
Job Corps (men)	97	68	3,840	5.2	738	.017	.09
NYC (women)	229	42	980	4.0	245	.098	.39
NYC (men)	150	60	980	4.0	245	.092	.37
CEP (Denver)	104	86	9,390	4.4	2134	.009	.04
WIN (Denver)	541	54	4,669	7.3	639	.063	.46
CEP (Richmond, CA.)	1019	74	7,823	b	b	.096	b
WIN (SF Bay Area)	749	43	10,119	11.9	850	.032	.38

[a] cost for each family (two trainees) for AJC

[b] data not available

1. total operating cost
   January 1972 through November 1973
   (from Table 5.3) $2,716,000
2. less .5 medical expenses
   for that period   (256,232)
3. operating costs attributable
   to AJC families for that period $2,459,768
4. average monthly operating costs
   (23 months)   106,946
5. average number of families during
   a month   79.7
6. average cost each family training
   month [(4) / (5)]   1,343
7. average cost each graduate training
   month (assuming 50 percent dropout rate)   2,686
8. average rehabilitation cost for each 1973
   AJC graduate-family [12 x (7)]   32,232

For the study sample graduates, the four-month follow-up study sample average of $6241 was used as the post-training salary. The unemployment rate was that found at the eight-month follow-up interview.

The cost for each trained family in the study sample uses the same eight-step procedure as was used for the 1973 graduates, except that the time period covered is the 27 months from February 1971 to April 1973, the time that the sample families were in training.

1. total operating cost
   (2/71 through 4/73) $2,669,800
2. less non-AJC medical expenses
   during that period   195,953
3. operating costs —AJC families $2,473,847
4. average monthly operating costs   91,624
5. average number of families   74.9
6. average cost for each family training-month   1,223
7. average cost for each graduate training-month
   (35 percent dropout rate)   1,882
8. average cost for each study sample graduate   22,584

The benefit/cost data for the Job Corps and NYC samples were transcribed directly from RMC (1969). The CEP and WIN were extracted from ORC (1971).

In 1970, the Denver CEP placed 213 trainees with an expenditure of $2,000,000, for a cost of $9,390 for each placed trainee (ORC 1971). The follow-up interviews revealed that CEP "graduates" had achieved a 5¢ gain in hourly wage over the average wages for the 12-month period prior to the training program and that 86 percent were employed (ORC 1971, Table 10.5).

The Denver WIN program expenditures for fiscal year 1969 amounted to $1,320,000 for which 239 job placements were made (ORC 1971). The cost of each job placement was therefore $5,523. The pre- to post-training wage increase was 46¢ an hour and the percent of time employed was 54 percent (ORC 1971).

The Richmond, California CEP placed 248 trainees in jobs at a cost of $1,940,114 in fiscal years 1969 and 1970; the average cost of each placement was therefore $7,823 (ORC 1971). The increase in wages resulting from the training experience amounted to 49¢ on the average, with 74 percent unemployment (ORC 1971).

The WIN program in the Bay Area achieved an increased wage of 36¢ and an employment rate of 43 percent for its 727 successful completions. The cost was $7,356,588 (ORC 1971), for a cost each completion of $10,119.

The data in Table 6.3 indicate that AJC is very successful and very expensive when compared with other Manpower programs. AJC graduates experience a significant increase in salary. However, for some of the less expensive programs, such as Job Corps, NYC, and CEP (Denver), it is difficult to imagine that the salary increases exhibited by the trainees would significantly change their level of living.

The statistics presented in Table 6.3 should be used with some caution. First, AJC is the only rural program in the analysis (except that some rural Job Corps and NYC programs are no doubt included in the national sample on which the data in RMC [1969] was based). The authors were unable to locate any comparable statistics on rural programs. Second, AJC trains families, so the training costs published for AJC in Table 6.3 is for 5.3 people on the average, 1.3 of whom are working adults (based on the 1973 AJC graduates).

This second point accounts for the relatively high employment rate for AJC's 1973 graduates. With more than one breadwinner in a trained unit, some redundancy against unemployment is present. In the 1973 graduates, for example, at the time of the follow-up contact, seven individuals were unemployed (three women and four men), but only three families were unemployed, that is, had no breadwinner employed. The 67 percent employment rate shown in Table 6.3 for study sample graduates was for husbands only - no doubt it would improve if working wives were considered. As was pointed out above, AJC's follow-up function was not active at the time the evaluation research team did their follow-up interviewing, which also accounts for the relatively (to 1973 graduates) lower employment rate for the study sample.

Figure 7 shows the benefits as a function of costs of placing a trained unit. The least-squares straightline fit of the points in the plot, the equation of which is

$$y = 783 + .108 \ (x-9646)$$

is also shown. Recall that the benefit used here is the difference between pre- and post-training annual salaries multiplied by the employment rate. One way of looking at these programs, therefore, is
that they are one of society's means of purchasing an increase in
gross national product. Figure 7 indicates that, within the bounds of
expenditures of the programs included in this analysis, the amount
of benefits that can be purchased by these programs is approximately
a linear function of the expenditure.

Figure 8 shows the benefit/cost ratios of the programs as a
function of costs. The benefit/cost ratio can be thought of as the program's efficiency in increasing GNP; it is the amount of increase for
each dollar spent. For example, NYC for women purchases a $.098
increase for each dollar spent at the $980 level, whereas AJC pur-
chases a $.113 increase for each dollar spent at the $32,232 level.
Therefore, the maximum achievable efficiency, which might be characterized by a straight-line fit in figure 8 through the NYC programs,
CEP-Richmond, and AJC, increases relatively slowly; this slow relative change accounts for the approximate linearity in Figure 7.

Summarizing the results of this section, AJC is significantly
more expensive on a cost each trained unit basis than the other manpower programs analyzed. However, the greater training costs for AJC
purchase considerably more benefits, and these benefits accrue at a
higher rate of efficiency than do those of the other programs.

Figure 9 presents the benefits plotted against the costs of a
trainee-month for the programs included in this analysis. The cost of
a trainee-month is a measure of the quality of training that a program
delivers. When viewed in this manner, AJC as a high-quality program
appears much more effective relative to other programs. There is,
however, some indication that the "law of diminishing returns" is in
effect over the $2000-$3000 range.

Figure 10 shows benefit/cost ratio B (see Table 6.3) against
the cost of a trainee-month. When viewed in this manner, AJC is much
more efficient in converting costs to benefits than are other programs.

The high benefits and high costs of AJC, when compared with
other programs, lead to the question, "How do AJC's various program
components contribute to the benefits derived from AJC?" A partial
answer to this question is possible from data presented earlier, in
Table 3.5. That table gives average salaries for AJC graduates who
were placed in both training-related and non-training-related jobs.
From the data in Table 3.5, assuming that the ratio of two-breadwinner
families to one-breadwinner families is the same as for the 1973 graduates, the average hourly salary for graduate-families placed in
non-training-related jobs is estimated to be $2.97. Assuming further
that vocational training is wasted on those families who are not placed
in training-related jobs, one can conclude that the vocational training
component contributes $0.81 an hour or $1685 a year of the increase,
while the remaining AJC components contribute between $1913 (for

FIGURE 7

Manpower Program Benefits as a Function of Costs

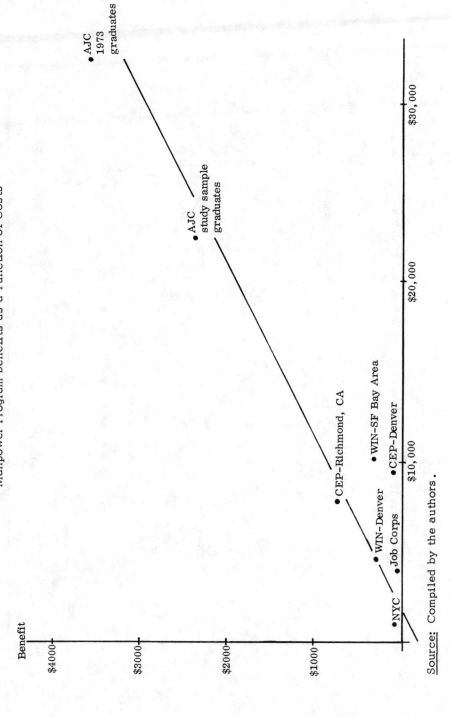

Source: Compiled by the authors.

FIGURE 8

Manpower Program Benefit/Cost Ratios as a Function of Costs

Source: compiled by the authors.

FIGURE 9

Manpower Program Benefits as a Function of Monthly Training Cost

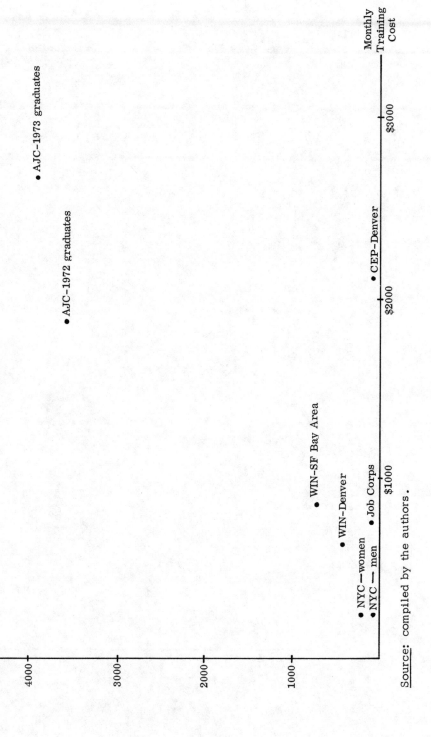

Source: compiled by the authors.

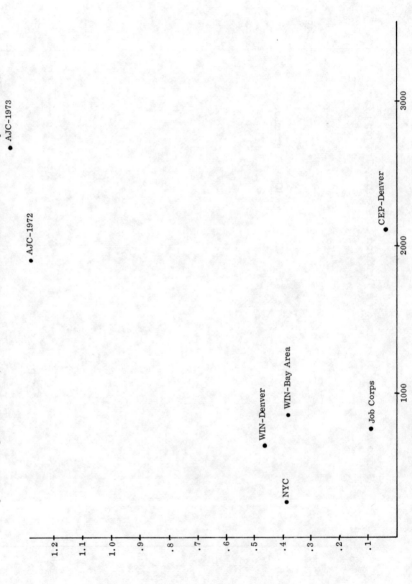

FIGURE 10

Manpower Program Benefit/Cost Ratio #2 as a Function of Monthly Training Cost

Source: compiled by the authors.

study sample graduates) and $2226 (for 1973 graduates). It is also evident that, for AJC, the presence of the non-vocational-training components create an "amplification effect" on that portion of the benefits attributable to vocational training alone, since the $1685 a year increase due to vocational training for AJC graduates exceeds the benefits for all the other programs examined.

There is another important point: for AJC's target population, AJC is the only program analyzed that creates enough economic gains for its trainees to move from below to above the poverty line. The best non-AJC program yielded benefits of $1019. A rural poor family trained in that program (CEP, Richmond, CA) would be expected to move from $2616 to $3635; the poverty to nonpoverty threshold for the average AJC target population family is $4925.

7

AJC'S ACCOMPLISHMENTS

Ultimately, an evaluation must come to grips with the question of whether the program in question was a success or not. Unfortunately, the usual case with a complex social program such as AJC is that many factors have to be considered and the results are generally mixed. The first step in determining whether the program was successful is to determine whether the program that was planned was indeed the program put into effect. Although AJC experienced some problems along the way, it was by and large very successful at implementing a comprehensive residential family rehabilitation program during the period in which it was funded by the office of Economic Opportunity (OEO). AJC had to overcome some formidable problems in implementing the program plan, three of which stand out. First, there was some initial communtiy opposition to locating AJC in Casa Grande. This resistance was overcome, even though litigation was involved, and the success of AJC and perhaps more importantly, its contribution to the local economy, made the community its staunch supporters.

AJC's second problem, and the most difficult one of its early years was the slow development of its residential housing. The bureaucratic delays and financial shenanigans of out-to-make-a-fast-buck developers caused AJC to incur major unanticipated expenses in having to develop alternative housing and a transportation system for the client-families until the residential housing was available. We would register here in passing a strong criticism of the Turnkey Housing Program, which enables developers to turn a fast buck by "selling" the rights to the project to each other at the project's expense while not building any houses for the poor. As practiced in Pinal County, one may ask whether the Turnkey Program was designed to enrich developers or to provide desperately-needed homes. Although the present study was never intended as a full-scale evaluation of the

Turnkey Housing Program and is limited to just one example, it seems clear that turnkey was a ripoff of the taxpayers' and of lower-income families to the extent it was sold to the public as a housing program for the poor.

AJC's third, and perhaps ultimately fatal problem in carrying out comprehensive residential family rehabilitation program involved the transfer of AJC from OEO to the Department of Labor (DOL) as a part of the Nixon administration's effort to destroy OEO. Although there were areas within DOL interested in the idea of comprehensive training programs, the dominant philosophy at DOL appeared to be one of providing the cheapest possible job training. Since ancillary services such as remedial education, daycare centers, and housing were not directly related to job training except to run up the price, they were to be avoided. Unfortunately, AJC was placed under an official at DOL who was adamantly against comprehensive programs. AJC was transferred to DOL just as the authors had finished data collection and were in the process of preparing the report on which this study is based. However, our informal observations of AJC during its first year under DOL lead to the conclusion that DOL, as a matter of policy, set out to destroy the comprehensive nature of AJC and to convert it into a typical Manpower Development and Training Act (MDTA: the largest DOL program) job-training program. Fortunately, AJC's multiple funding sources gave it a source of countervailing power which may enable it to resist DOL's desires. At the time of writing, however, the outcome was in doubt.

There was only one area in which AJC failed to implement at least a good approximation of the original plan during the period under study. Originally, the idea was that AJC would be mobile, setting up operations in an area for a limited period of time during which the resident poor of that area would be trained for jobs available locally. After the local pool of poor was exhausted, AJC would pack up its house trailers and move its operation to another area where the process would be repeated. Ideally, AJC would leave behind a more viable rural community than when it arrived, not only by attacking rural poverty and stimulating the local economy by providing needed skilled workers, but also by leaving behind a legacy of social action and community involvement and public housing. This did not happen, and, for the foreseeable future, AJC will be stuck in Casa Grande.

Several factors contributed to the failure to develop a migrating AJC. First, the struggle for simple survival in the face of OEO funding cutbacks, DOL hostility, and the increasing difficulties in finding alternative sources for funds in a declining economy shifted AJC's attention away from the yet-to-be-accomplished parts of the grand scheme. The transfer of AJC first from OEO's office of Program Development to OEO's Migrant Program and then to DOL's Migrant Program had a subtle but important effect on AJC's future. As originally planned and put into operation, AJC served all the poor in a relatively limited

geographic area, in keeping with the scheme of the mobile job college.
When AJC began receiving funds under OEO's migrant program, it was
required to have at least 50 percent migrant enrollment and was under
continuous pressure from OEO and later from DOL to increase the proportion of migrants. Since AJC was enrolling less than 50 percent
migrants at the time of the first transfer, AJC had to either increase
migrant recruiting within western Pinal County or expand its service
area or move to a different location. To move the job college at that
juncture would have been ill-timed, since AJC had not completed its
service to Pinal County. Further, these changes came at a time when
AJC's struggle for funds was particularly desperate. To have embarked
on a major new direction - moving and reestablishing the job colleges -
would have been financial folly. So AJC turned to increased migrant
recruitment, which was only partially successful. In addition, DOL
and the OEO Migrants Program were philosophically opposed to the
idea of a limited geographic service area and were constantly press-
uring AJC to expand to statewide service. Eventually, AJC gave in.

    The failure to establish a mobile training program was not en-
tirely due to outside forces. AJC underestimated the problems involved
in developing such a program, especially with regard to bureaucratic
inertia and vested interests. Once AJC became a viable institution with
ties to the community and especially with a staff who came to see
Casa Grande as home, the difficulty of overcoming the inertia to stay
in Casa Grande became increasingly great. The problems of getting
the housing program set up and of financing AJC, along with the daily
burden of administering the program, continually diverted the attention of the administration away from the establishment of a mobile job
college. Since that was something that would happen at some unspeci-
fied time in the future, it was a task that could be, and was, put off
until tomorrow. As AJC settled into Casa Grande and as planning the
move was put out of mind, the conception of the mobile job college
began to fade until, at last, it seems to have disappeared.

    Given that AJC was successful in developing the kind of pro-
gram it set out to establish, the next question is whether the program
worked well enough so that it was reasonable to expect the program
to have produced positive results. The discussion in Chapter 3 indicates that AJC was generally very successful in its program operations. The final test is whether the results of the program operations
were those desired. Table 7.1 summarizes the findings of the family
interviews for program evaluation measures. In general, AJC was
quite successful in improving the economic, attitudinal, and lifestyle
status of its client-families.

    Some of the areas where no improvement was noticed deserve
comment. The various measures of participation in formal group activities indicate only a small increase. AJC laid fairly heavy emphasis
on getting people involved in such activities, so the small change may
not indicate much success on AJC's part in this area. On the other
hand, Americans are not as great a nation of joiners as the popular

TABLE 7.1

Summary of Family Interview Evaluation Variables

Measure	Statistically Significant Gain	Gain (Not Significant)	No Change	Loss (Not Significant)	Statistically Significant Loss
Union membership					
PTA membership		x			
Church attendance			x		
Composite group memberships		x			
Registered to vote	x				
Achieving goals	x				
Optimism about future			x		
Hadley Cantril Self-anchoring Scale	x				
Having a checking account	x				
Size of savings account	x				
Annual income (family)	x				
Per capita income	x				
Number of debts		x			
Amount of indebtedness				x	
Ratio of debts to income					
Job Satisfication Index	x				
Family scale			x		
Semantic Differentials				x	
Alienation (Nettler Scale)				x	
Expect children to go to college					x
Home ownership	x				
Number of rooms per person	x				
Value of cars and trucks	x				
Owned a vehicle			x		
Food expenditures			x		

myth would lead one to believe. Our observations lead us to believe
that AJC overemphasized this part of the American dream and set its
goal of making everyone a joiner too high.

The indebtedness of the families increased. Although not de-
sirable, the increase must be looked at in the proper frame of reference.
For the year prior to entering AJC, the average family indebtedness was
80 percent of annual income. For the post-program period, indebtedness,
although increasing in absolute terms, showed a striking decline to 54
percent of annual income. It would seem that the families' greater indebtedness after the program is due to their improved economic status.
Whether their level of debt is still too high or not, they are clearly
better able to afford their post-program debt than they were able to
afford their pre-AJC level of debt.

The slight but not statistically significant decrease in scores
on the Semantic Differential items may be accounted for by a recent
finding by Block (1975). In a study of psychological well-being in four
manpower training programs —MDTA, Job Opportunities in the Business
Sector (JOBS: another DOL program), Job Corps, and NYC—Block found
a marked elevation in the level of psychological well-being during early
weeks in the program. This high level of affect seems best explained
as a case of high hopes and expectations of a better future. Entry into
the training program raised the trainees' hopes, and excited them. One
year after completing the program, psychological well-being had returned
to or even dropped below the level of a control group. This is accounted
for by the failure of the programs to live up to the trainees' expectations.
When they found that going through the programs made little difference
in their lives, their overall level of psychological satisifaction returned
to its prior state. Although the scale used by Block was different from
those used in the AJC evaluation, there is enough overlap in their content areas to expect the same phenomena to have occurred in the AJC
families. It is our hypothesis then that entry into AJC produced a revo-
lution of rising expectations in the client-families. When the families
were interviewed during their first days at AJC, the affective measures
reflected this elevated level rather than measuring their true pre-program
level. It is interesting to note that Block's measure showed a decline
of eight standard deviations in the initial measure to the one year after
the program post-test. We must point out to readers without a background in statistics that a decline of this size can only be described
as staggering. If we assume that Block's measure and the AJC Semantic
Differential items and Nettler's Alienation Scale overlap in ther content
domains to some degree, the small decline in the AJC measures compared
to the huge drop in Block's population suggests that AJC was relatively
successful in bringing about the desired attitudinal changes. In other
words, based on Block's results, a much greater drop in the AJC measures
would have been expected than was actually found.

The AJC parents' expectations of their children going to college
are also consistent with the theory advanced in the preceding paragraph.

Upon entry into AJC, 80 percent of the parents expected their children to attend college. This is grossly unrealistic for a rural poor population. The decrease in this expectation between the first measure and the post-program interview may be indicative of the return of affective states to a more realistic level.

Returning to Table 7.1, we see that the AJC families were generally better off after their AJC experience than before. Does this mean that AJC and comprehensive residential family training programs are a good thing? There are two major problems in answering this question from the present data. Although the same difficulties hold for all the measures, only family income will be discussed because it illustrates the problems and is probably the single most important measure of the program's success.

The AJC families had higher incomes after going through AJC than they had before the AJC training, but how do we know that the increase was due to AJC training? During the same time, the economy was changing, people were moving in and out of Pinal County, new jobs were opening, some jobs were being lost, and other changes were taking place. Perhaps these changes in the local and national economy alone would have resulted in a finding of increased income if one had just found a group of poor families, measured their income, and then measured it again two years later. The best way to deal with this problem is by the use of control groups—a sample of families similar to those who entered AJC but who did not receive any training. AJC was not designed to include a control group. While this was unfortunate, little would be gained by going into a lengthy criticism of why this should not have been done. Rather, we will try to find the answer from what we have.

Recall that AJC, in its planning period, conducted a survey of the rural poor of Pinal County. (The AJC survey is described in the next section.) In order to approximate a control group, the evaluation sought to reinterview those people included in the AJC survey who still lived in Pinal County and who had not enrolled in AJC. This reinterview effort was carried out at the same time the post-program interviews were being conducted. Unfortunately, the limited budget for the evaluation study necessitated some cost-saving acts. In particular, the reinterviews were conducted largely with families listed in the telephone directory. Although using the phone book makes it easier and cheaper to find these families, this procedure introduces a bias into the data; the families chosen will be economically better off than those who can't afford a telephone. However, this bias is not necessarily a problem. If the AJC families' income gain was greater than the gain for the telephone directory families, then it must be greater than that of those too poor to afford a telephone. Over a four year period (1968-72) the 54 families contacted in the telephone survey gained $79 per year, compared to the AJC families' $1618 annual increase.

Another semi-control-group can be created using Morgan, et al. (1974) who studied the income changes of 5,000 families over five years, from 1967 to 1971. Only poor families were taken, and they showed an average annual increase of $292 (Morgan et al. 1974, p.70). The AJC families had an average annual income of $1,618. Although the two populations are not entirely comparable, one being a national sample of the poor while the other was a sample of rural poor families, there is no prior reason to expect these demographic differences to account for such a difference in income.

It was pointed out above that perhaps one mechanism by which AJC raised incomes was by increasing the number of wage-earners in the family. Wives who were unemployable were taught job skills, and family attitudes against working wives were modified. Again, the data from the study of 5,000 families can be used for comparison. According to Morgan et al. (1974, p. 43) those families with an increased number of wage-earners and more family members (that the relatively young AJC families were growing is to be expected) had an annual average increase in income of 38 percent. The AJC families increased their income by 66 percent per year.

Although the study lacked a proper control group, the evidence supports the conclusion that AJC was effective in increasing the families' income. The AJC families did better than the poor families in general. The AJC families did better than growing poor families with more wage earners. The AJC families did better than similar families from the same county in a comparison that was loaded against AJC. Finally, a change in average income from $2,392 for the year before AJC to $5,529 is just too big to explain away as due to "other factors."

Unfortunately, similar comparative data is not available for the noneconomic measures. Their interpretation has to be based only on the pre/post change and the fact that other comparisons indicate that AJC caused a real change in income, which implies the other changes may also be due to AJC.

The second problem in trying to decide if AJC was a good thing is related to the complexity of the AJC program. The various components of AJC can be divided into two functionally very different categories - training/rehabilitation and job placement. The problem is to determine whether the economic success observed in the AJC families was only a result of AJC finding them good jobs, or did the rest of the program contribute anything? Again, the design of AJC and of the evaluation make a clear-cut answer to this question impossible. (In order to deal with this issue directly, a group of families would have to go through the AJC training and then find jobs on their own). The best evidence available bearing on this question is the income differential between AJC graduates who had training-related jobs and those who didn't. That placement in a training-related job resulted in $1,685 a year more income on the average is reasonably good evidence that training did make a difference.

In summary, AJC seems to have been fairly successful in accomplishing its aims. The lives of its client-families were improved and the extent of the improvement exceeded the changes in their lives one would otherwise have expected. Does this also mean comprehensive family residential training programs are a good idea? Since the issue is whether adding the other program components results in an improvement beyond what would have resulted only from vocational training, the $1,913 income increase for those in non-training-related jobs suggests that the additional program components had an impact. That this increase is greater than the $1,685 per year attributable to job-related training suggests that the nonvocational components may even be the most important. The absolute amounts of these figures should be treated with some skepticism since they are not correct for economic growth—the control group problem—nor for the contribution of AJC's job placement program. However, the relative contributions of the two program components are of some interest.

Two different philosophies in antipoverty programs can be identified.* The first is exclusively an economic approach which assumes that the problem of poverty in the midst of plenty is due to a mismatch between the jobs available in the economy and the work skills possessed by the unemployed; the unemployed will, according to this approach, be able to find work if they are given the proper skills—hence, the various manpower training programs. The alternative philosophy holds that simple skill training is not enough. In order to break the poverty cycle, a number of aspects of the family's life style, attitudes, and motivation must be changed. The findings of the AJC evaluation lend some support to the second theory. The greater income effect of the nonjob training components and AJC's superior performance when compared to traditional job training programs suggests there is much to be said in favor of comprehensive residential family rehabilitation programs.

SELECTION EFFECTS

An important question to ask of any social welfare program is whether it is delivering its services and benefits to the intended population. In the case of a program like AJC where those services are intended to have future consequences of improving the clients' economic,

---

*It is only fair to note that both philosophies assume that jobs are available. This assumption is probably the most serious error in the conceptualization of the various antipoverty programs. The reader is invited to imagine how different the war on poverty would have been if it began with the assumption that the basic problem was the failure of the economy to provide enough jobs for the population.

social and psycological well-being, it is necessary to determine
whether the families taken into the program are representative of the
poor. If the program's selection procedures operate in such a fashion
as to select into the program families who would have a better than
average chance of breaking out of poverty on their own without any
program imput (a phenomenon called "creaming"), a program that had
no effect may appear to be effective because its clients did improve
on the relevant measures, but only because of the kind of people they
were, not because of what the program did for them.

        We can address the question of whether AJC's selection system
"creams" or not by comparing the characteristics of the families enrolled
in AJC to the characteristics of the families surveyed by AJC in 1968.
AJC, before beginning operations, conducted a survey of the Pinal
County poverty population to gather more detailed information on the
need for such a program than could be learned from census data. The
AJC survey gives more detailed information on the characteristics of
the poverty population of Pinal County than does the census data.

        A note of caution on the AJC survey procedure must be made.
Interviewers went to known poverty pockets in the county and attempted
a 100 percent sample of the residents. About 800 persons were interviewed. It cannot be determined whether this sampling procedure
resulted in a representative sample of the Pinal County poor. Table 7.2
shows the variables for which data was available for AJC families upon
entry and for those who met the AJC eligibility criteria from the AJC
survey of the Pinal County poor. The following differences were noted:

- AJC families are considerably younger than those surveyed
  in 1968
- because of the difference in age, AJC families average fewer
  children than their 1968 survey counterparts
- AJC families worked more weeks during the year than those
  surveyed in 1968
- AJC families are better-educated than respondents to the
  1968 survey
- because they are younger, AJC families have younger children
- the distribution of the ethnic backgrounds of AJC families
  differs from that observed in the 1968 survey; AJC was not
  able to attract enough Black families to match the proportion
  (25 percent) indicated by that survey

        When examined by individual ethnic groups, the differences
are less evident. All AJC groups are younger, which accounts for all
other differences.

        There is an apparent anomaly in the data shown in Table 7.2
which suggests that, although the AJC families had less unemployment
than the AJC-eligible families in the AJC survey, their income was

TABLE 7.2

Comparison of AJC Family Characteristics to Families in 1968
Survey of Pinal County Poor Eligible for AJC

Characteristics	All Ethnic Groups		Indian Only		Black Only		Anglo Only		Mexican-American Only	
	All AJC Families	All Pinal County Families	AJC	Pinal Cty	AJC	Pinal Cty	AJC	Pinal Cty	AJC	Pinal Cty
Mean age of male head of household	30.1	39.5[b]	24.5	31.8[b]	21.7	40.6[b]	30.3	41.7[b]	32.1	39.0[b]
Mean number of weeks worked in last year	41.6	37.1[a]	42.9	42.2	38.2	31.7	38.4	31.7	42.8	40.6
Mean number of children	3.0	4.3[b]	2.3	3.8	2.3	3.6	2.5	4.2	3.4	4.6[b]
Mean annual earnings	$2620	$2680	$2240	$2690	$1720	$2420	$2590	$2290	$2810	$2900
Ethnic background (percent)										
Indian	9.5	4[b]	--	--	--	--	--	--	--	--
Black	8.5	22	--	--	--	--	--	--	--	--
Anglo	20.0	18	--	--	--	--	--	--	--	--
Mexican-American	62.0	56	--	--	--	--	--	--	--	--
Percent speak english at home	96.0	91	NA	NA	NA	NA	NA	NA	84	86
Percent on welfare	12	11	10	0	11	7	5	17	15	10
Percent with previous training	27	25	30	13	33	22	35	31	25	25
Age of oldest child										
less than 6	54	24[b]	70	31	67	25[a]	47	23	52	22[b]
6 – 12	27	28	30	38	33	28	29	32	25	27
13 – 16	9	22	0	6	0	25	19	24	8	21
more than 16	10	26	0	25	0	22	5	21	15	30
Years education for family head (percent)										
1 – 4	22	30[a]	0	19	0	17[b]	14	14	31	42
5 – 9	43	48	50	50	11	49	57	61	41	43
more than 9	35	22	50	31	89	34	29	25	28	15
n =	105	386	10	16	9	83	21	70	65	217

[a]Difference between AJC and Pinal County values significant at P < .05
[b]Difference between AJC and Pinal County values significant at P < .01

about the same. This finding is probably due to the difference in age of the head-of-household in the two groups. Earnings increase with age, and this increase in income associated with the greater age of the non-AJC families probably offset the increased income earned by the AJC families due to their higher education and their greater employment.

Three findings in Table 7.2 are important in answering the question of whether AJC "creamed" the Pinal County poverty population. When compared to the general poverty population of Pinal County who meet AJC's eligibility criteria, the families attending AJC are younger, better educated, and more likely to be employed. Being younger, their future incomes are likely to rise faster than the income of the general population as they approach their peak earnings period. Being better educated, they are likely to earn more than comparable families of the same age with less education, and having less unemployment (which may be a result of their greater education), they should earn more. In short, the future looks somewhat better for AJC families than it does for the general population of Pinal County poor because of the characteristics AJC families bring with them into the program.

This finding raises a note of caution in interpreting the findings of the rest of the study, for it suggests that the AJC families will show some improvement in their life situation in the future simply because of the way they were selected. However, it does not seem likely that these differences would account for all the improvement observed in the AJC families. For instance, the average weekly wage for weeks worked for the survey families was $84, compared to $63 for the AJC families. If we assign all this difference to the fact that the AJC family heads were younger and therefore still to achieve their peak earnings period, which the survey families were closer to, the $21 a week difference in income is only $2.23 a week for each year of difference in age between the AJC and Pinal County families. On an annual basis, age would raise the AJC families income $116, or only about 10 percent of the $1618 annual income increment actually experienced.

In conclusion, AJC can be criticized somewhat for selecting its program people from the poverty population who stand a little better chance for the future due to their present stage in the family cycle. However, it is very doubtful that this "creaming" effect can account for all the gains realized by the AJC families.

TESTS AND PROCEDURES USED AT AJC'S
TESTING AND VOCATIONAL EVALUATION UNIT

The following list of tests, work samples, and materials is offered in an attempt to illustrate the specific instruments from which selections were made to meet the needs of an individual in evaluation.

Intelligence
Weschsler Adult Intelligence Scale (WAIS)
Raven Progressive Matrices
Peabody Picture Vocabulary Test

Personality
Minnesota Multiphasic Personality Inventory
16 PF
House-Tree-Person
Hand Test
Rotter Incomplete Sentence Blank

Interest
Strong Vocational Interest Blank
Minnesota Vocational Interest Inventory
Picture Interest Inventory

Achievement
Wide Range Achievement Test
Wide Range Vocabulary Test
California Achievement Test Battery
College Qualifying Test
Army General Classification Test
Gates-MacGinitie Reading Test Series
Adult Basic Learning Examination

Aptitude
General Clerical Test
Minnesota Clerical Test
Revised Minnesota Paper Form Board
Bennett Mechanical Test
O'Rourke Mechanical Test
Aptitude for Nursing Test
Watson-Glaser Critical Thinking

Accounting Orientation Test
Aptitude Test for Programmer Personnel
Purdue Blueprint Reading Test
Purdue Trade Information Test for Sheetmetal Workers
Purdue Trade Information Test in Welding
Purdue Information Test for Carpentry
Purdue Mechanical Adaptability Test
Purdue Non-Language Personnel Test
Purdue Clerical Adaptability Test

Dexterity
Purdue Pegboard Test
Minnesota Rate of Manipulation Test
O'Connor Fine Finger Dexterity Test
Crawford Small Parts Dexterity Test
Minnesota Spatial Relation Test
Bennett Mechanical Hand Tool Test
Pennsylvania Bi-Manual Dexterity Test
Stromberg Dexterity Test

Visual and Hearing
Titmus Occupational Vision Screening
Titmus Audiogram

Job Sampling
Drawing
Drafting
Money Handling
Filing and Alphabetizing
Typing
Kelly Clerical
Clerical #8
Clerical #5
Business Arithmetic I
Business Arithmetic II
Inventory
Arithmetic Diagnostic Battery
Business Spelling
Abbreviations
Basic Skills
Telephone Directory
Measuring
Wright Post Office
Wood Clamp Assembly and Disassembly
Valpar I
Valpar II
Sickels Color and Symbol Discrimination

      Small Engine
      Lesem Lighter
      Curnett Teacher Aide
      Catalog Exercise
      Daily Living Skills
      Sewing
      Cooking

Shop Task

Individualized tasks selected specifically to meet the needs of that individual.

Job Exploration

      Dictionary of Occupational Titles
      Occupational Outlook Handbook
      Employment Security Commission Pamphlets
      Personal Interview

Organic Involvement

      Bender-Gestalt
      Hooper Visual Organization Test
      Minnesota Test for Differential Diagnosis of Aphasia
      Exam for Aphasia
      Hunt-Minnesota Test for Organic Brain Damage
      Harris Test for Lateral Dominance
      Frostig Development Test of Visual Perception
      Trail Making
      Psychoeducational Inventory of Basic Learning Abilities
      Illinois Test of Psycholinguistic Abilities (ITPA)
      Arthur Point Scale of Performance Tests, Form II

VOCATIONAL TRAINING COURSES
OFFERED THROUGH AJC

Key to Training Sites:
        Ac. of Drafting – Academy of Drafting
        AJC – Arizona Job Colleges, Inc.
        CAC – Central Arizona College
        EIA – Electronics Institute of Arizona
        GRCC – Gila River Career Center
        LBC – Lamson Business College
        MCSC – Maricopa County Skill Center
        Rock. Inst. – Rockland Institute
        RSI – Refrigeration Schools, Inc.
        UTI – Universal Technical Institute

Training	Training Site	Time Involved
Automotive Service		
Arts and Crafts, Commercial	GRCC	4 hrs. a day/16 weeks
Auto Parts Sales Clerk	GRCC	4 hrs. a day/16 weeks
Automotive Air-Conditioning	U.T.I.	6 hrs. a day/3 weeks
Automotive Mechanics	U.T.I.	6 hrs. a day/21 weeks
Automotive Mechanics	GRCC	4 hrs. a day/10–12 weeks
Brake and Front End Specialist	GRCC	4 hrs. a day/*
Bus Mechanic	GRCC	4 hrs. a day/*
Diesel Engines	GRCC	4 hrs. a day/*
Diesel Engines	U.T.I.	6 hrs. a day/9 weeks
Foreign Car Repair	U.T.I.	6 hrs. a day/6 weeks
Tune–Up Mechanic	GRCC	4 hrs. a day/*
	U.T.I.	6 hrs. a day/9 weeks
Building Maintenance Worker		
Building Maintenance Worker	AJC	4 hrs. a day/24 weeks
Building Trades		
Carpentry	GRCC	4 hrs. a day/24–32 weeks
Masonry	GRCC	4 hrs. a day/40 weeks

---

*length dependent on amount of time needed to reach proficiency

Training	Training Site	Time Involved
Child Care		
Child Care Aide	AJC	4-7 hrs. a day/24 weeks
Culinary Arts		
Cook's Helper	AJC	4-7 hrs. a day/24 weeks
Cook	GRCC	6 hrs. a day/36-52 weeks
Food Service Worker	GRCC	4 hrs. a day/*
Dental Assistant		
Dental Assistant	Blair College	6-8 hrs. a day/40 weeks
Dental Assistant	Bryman Schools	4 hrs. a day/16 weeks
Drafting		
Drafting	Ac. of Drafting	6 hrs. a day/16-52 weeks
Electrical Service		
Electrician	GRCC	4 hrs. a day/24-32 weeks
Electronics		
Electronics Technician	EIA	6 hrs. a day/52 weeks
Radio and TV Repairman	GRCC	4 hrs. a day/52 weeks
Home Health Aide		
Home Health Aide	AJC	8 hrs. a day/24-36 weeks
Law Enforcement		
Correctional Officer	CAC	8 hrs. a day/24 weeks
Meat Cutting		
Meat Cutter	MCSC	6-8 hrs. a day/24 weeks
Medical Assistant		
Medical Assistant	Blair College	
Medical Assistant	Bryman Schools	4 hrs. a day/28 weeks
Needletrades		
Needletrades	GRCC	4 hrs. a day/12-24 weeks

---

*length dependent on amount of time needed to reach proficiency

Training	Training Site	Time Involved
Nurse's Aide		
Nurse's Aide	GRCC	6 hrs. a day/24-36 weeks
Office Administration		
Accounting	LBC	8 hrs. a day/*
Business Administration	LBC	8 hrs. a day/*
Business Management	CAC	8 hrs. a day/52 weeks
Clerk Typist	GRCC	4 hrs. a day/28 weeks
Complete Office Machines	LBC	8 hrs. a day/*
Computer Programming	Rock. Inst.	8 hrs. a day/*
IBM Key Punch	LBC	8 hrs. a day/*
IBM Key Punch	Rock. Inst.	8 hrs. a day/*
Office Administration	Rock. Inst.	8 hrs. a day/*
PBX Receptionist	LBC	8 hrs. a day/*
Stenographer	GRCC	4 hrs. a day/40 weeks
Stenographer	LBC	8 hrs. a day/*
Refrigeration		
Commercial and Domestic		
Refrigeration, Air Condition-	U.T.I.	6 hrs. a day/27 weeks
ing, and Heating	RSI	6 hrs. a day/20 weeks
Welding		
Welding	GRCC	4 hrs. a day/40-52 weeks

---

*length dependent on amount of time needed to reach proficiency

AJC HEALTH SERVICES DIVISION ENCOUNTERS,
FISCAL YEAR 1973

A. Clinic Visits	11,103	
B. Referred Out	1,811	
C. Dental Visits	437	
D. Total Encounters with Facility	12,223	(an average of 47 each day)

1. Family Planning Clinics   276 (encounters with individuals)
2. Well Child Care (Immunization)   3,358 (1,083 children)
3. Parental Care   574 (92 individuals)
4. T.B. Testing   1,264 individuals
5. Lab Visits   3,406
6. AJC Pharmacy   16,465
7. Outside Pharmacy   1,149
8. Vision Screening   364
9. Auditory Screening   356
10. Screening Chest X-Ray   291
11. Home Health Aide Visits   2,994
12. Individual Health Counseling
    (Home Health Aide)   375
13. Health Classes   442 individuals
14. Total Home Health Aide
    Home Visits   3,369 (3,672 individuals)
15. Home Health Aide
    Visits to Camps to Recruit   528
16. Total Travel by Department   154,000 miles
17. Travel by Home Health Aide   89,104
18. Travel-Transfer Patients   64,869
19. Total Number of Families Served   756
20. Total Number of People Served   4,576
21. AJC Families Served   221
22. AJC People Served   1,149
23. Migrant and Seasonal Farm
    Workers, Families   535
24. Migrant and Seasonal Farm
    Workers, Total People   3,427

AJC 1969. Proposal for a Vocational and Educational Training Program. Casa Grande, Ariz.: Arizona Job Colleges, Inc., mimeograph.

Amex Civil Systems 1973. An Evaluation of Arizona Job Colleges Incorporated (sic). El Segundo, Ca.: Amex Civil Systems.

Aries Corp. 1974. A Survey of Rehabilitative-Type Programs in the Mountain Plains States. NIE Contract # OEC-0-72-5240. Washington, D. C.: National Institue of Education.

Becker, G. S. 1964. Human Capital. New York: Columbia University Press.

Block, A. H. 1975. A Preliminary Assessment of the Relationship of ABS and Participants Experience In Manpower Training Programs. HEW Contract No. OS-74-186. Washington, D. C.: Team Associates, Inc.

Cantril, H. 1965. The Pattern of Human Concerns. New Brunswick, N. J.: Rutgers University Press.

Ferman, L. A., Kornbluh, S. L., and Haber, A., eds. 1965. Poverty In America. Ann Arbor, Mich.: University of Michigan Press.

Litwin, G. and Stringer, R. A., Jr. 1968. Motivation and Organizational Climate. Cambridge, Mass.: Harvard University Press.

March, M. S. 1968. The Neighborhood Center Concept. Public Welfare 26 (April): 97-111.

Morgan, J. N., Dickinson, K., Dickinson, J., Benus, J., and Duncan, G. 1974. Five Thousand American Families: Patterns of Economic Progress. Ann Arbor, Mich.: Institute for Social Research.

Nau, L. 1973. Why Not Family Rehabilitation. Journal of Rehabilitation (May-June) 42: 14-17.

---1973b. Family Rehabilitation in Process. Rehabilitation Record 14 (Sept. - Oct.): 8-11.

Nettler, G. 1957. A Measure of Alienation. American Sociological
    Review 22: 670-77.

ORC 1971. The Total Impact of Manpower Programs: A Four City Case
    Study. Vol. II - Final Report. Washington, D. C.; Olympus
    Research Corp.

RMC 1969. Evaluations of the War on Poverty: The Feasibility of
    Benefit-Cost Analysis for Manpower Programs. Resource
    Management Corp. Washington, D. C.: U. S. Government
    Printing Office, #183305.

SSS 1971. Arizona Job Colleges, Inc. First Year Evaluation. Office of
    Economic Opportunity Contract # BOO-5192. Washington, D. C.:
    Office of Economic Opportunity.

Stephenson, J. B. 1968. Shiloh, A Mountain Community. Lexington,
    Ky.: University of Kentucky Press.

Storm, J. 1972. Economic Analysis of Casa Grande, Ariz. Phoenix,
    Ariz.: Planning Division, Department of Economic Planning and
    Development, state of Arizona.

Time 1972. Split Views on America. Time December 25, 1972, pp.
    12-13.

KEITH BAKER is a Social Science Analyst in the Office of the
Assistant Secretary for Planning and Evaluation, Department of Health,
Education, and Welfare; he has also worked on the evaluation staff
at the Office of Economic Opportunity. In addition to publishing several
articles in noted journals, Dr. Baker is coauthor of Prison Education.
He received his B.A. from Miami University, and his M.A. and Ph. D.
in Sociology from the University of Wisconsin.

MYFANWAY GLASSO is currently a scientific editor at General
Atomic Co. She was principal investigator on the Arizona Job Colleges
evaluation research project for the first three years. She has participated in several social and educational research and development projects for both public and private institutions. She received her B.A.
in English Literature from San Diego State University.

DONALD R. GOYETTE is vice president of Policy Development
Corporation. He has participated in a number of social program evaluations, primarily being responsible for data processing and statistical
analysis. He received his A.B. from the University of California at
Los Angeles.

C. FREMONT SPRAGUE is president of Policy Development Corporation.
He has participated in several projects concerned with evaluating social
programs, primarily in the areas of research methodology, cost analysis,
and general project management. He has served in these capacities as
a staff member of several contract research firms and has worked on
projects funded by the Office of Economic Opportunity, the U. S.
Department of Housing and Urban Development, and the Bureau of
Indian Affairs. He received his Ph.D. in Operations Research from
Case Western Reserve University, his M.S. in Mathematics from the
University of New Mexico, and his B.S. in Mathematics from Oklahoma
State University.

AN EVALUATION OF POLICY-RELATED
REHABILITATION RESEARCH
Monroe Berkowitz, Valerie Englander,
Jeffrey Rubin, and John D. Worrall

MINORITY ACCESS TO FEDERAL GRANTS-IN-AID:
The Gap Between Policy and Performance
John Hope II

POLITICIZING THE POOR: The Legacy of the War
on Poverty in a Mexican-American Community
Biliana C. S. Ambrecht

THE WELFARE FAMILY AND MASS ADMINISTRATIVE
JUSTICE
Daniel J. Baum